Learn Chess

John Nunn

First published in the UK by Gambit Publications Ltd 2000
Reprinted 2000, 2004, 2010 (with revisions and corrections), 2011, 2012, 2013, 2015
Copyright © John Nunn 2000, 2010
The right of John Nunn to be identified as the author of this work has been asserted in accordance with the Copyright, Designs and Patents Act 1988.

ISBN-13: 978-1-901983-30-2
ISBN-10: 1-901983-30-7

DISTRIBUTION:
Worldwide (except USA): Central Books Ltd, 99 Wallis Rd, London E9 5LN, England.
Tel +44 (0)20 8986 4854 Fax +44 (0)20 8533 5821.
E-mail: orders@Centralbooks.com

Gambit Publications Ltd, 99 Wallis Rd, London E9 5LN, England.
E-mail: info@gambitbooks.com
Website (regularly updated): www.gambitbooks.com

Edited by Graham Burgess and typeset by John Nunn
Printed in the USA by Bang Printing, Brainerd, Minnesota

10 9 8

Gambit Publications Ltd
Directors: Dr John Nunn GM, Murray Chandler GM and Graham Burgess FM
German Editor: Petra Nunn WFM

Contents

Introduction

This book aims to teach the basics of chess without assuming any prior knowledge of the game. This is hardly an original concept, so I will take a little time to outline how this book differs from others covering similar ground.

The style is intentionally no-nonsense. You will not find any gimmicks in these pages – only useful information. The various topics are covered at a comfortable pace. Many chess books for beginners speed rapidly through the basics before reaching the advanced material which the author finds interesting. I have attempted to avoid this trap, which is akin to starting a mathematics textbook with 1+1=2 and rushing on to Einstein's theory of relativity. Because of this, the range of topics covered is perhaps slightly restricted, but I hold the view that it is better to have a solid knowledge of a few key ideas than a tenuous and uncertain grasp of many, less important, concepts. I have concentrated on simple, practical advice – what you actually need to know to win games. Theory can wait until later, when you have built up your confidence and are seeking to progress further.

The world of chess has changed dramatically thanks to the availability of computers and the Internet. The use of computers is covered in some detail, and I have indicated how to start exploring the various chess resources available on the Internet.

One of my pet hates is the choice of games for beginners' books. There are certain standard examples that tend to be repeated in book after book. In many beginners' books, you will find the game Morphy vs Count Isouard and the Duke of Brunswick, played during a performance of the Paris Opera in 1858. It's not an especially good game, as one might expect when the strongest player of his day confronts two duffers. Moreover, it has always seemed to me faintly incredible that authors couldn't find a relevant example less than 150 years old. In this book, every game and game extract is from after 1900 (indeed, only two are earlier than 1950). The style of chess played today is quite different from that of 1858, and while some of the differences are subtle, there is no reason why players should not be exposed to contemporary chess thought from the beginning.

Chess is a wonderful pastime which has been enjoyed by millions of people all over the world for almost one and a half millennia. My book will have succeeded in its objective if it encourages you to join the ever-expanding community of chess-players.

John Nunn
Chertsey, April 2010

1 Why Learn Chess?

Chess is a game with a long history. Historians do not completely agree on the origins of chess, but generally accepted documentary evidence goes back to AD 800. Earlier than this, the disagreements begin. Only a handful of specific references survive, and these indicate that chess was already being played in India round about AD 600. Of course, chess may go back further than this, but in the absence of any real evidence this is pure speculation. Part of the difficulty in pinpointing the origins of chess stems from humanity's general fondness for board games. The 64-square board on which chess is played certainly goes back long before AD 600, but it was used for other games besides chess. Paintings in Egyptian tombs show that board games were being played round about 2500 BC, and actual pieces have been found from Roman times. However, no Egyptian king thought to have a rule book inscribed in his tomb, and practically nothing is known about the rules of these very early games. It is therefore impossible to say whether they were the ancestors of chess or some other modern game.

After AD 800, the main source of information regarding chess comes from the Arab world. Written records become more common, composed chess puzzles start to appear and there is even some analysis of relevance to over-the-board play. The rules of the game were somewhat different then, but the moves of the king, rook and knight were essentially the same as in the modern game. Some 13th century Arabic analysis of the ending king and rook vs king and knight is therefore still relevant today. Recently, it has become possible to check this analysis by using a computer database; it stands up surprisingly well after a time-span of more than 700 years. By this time, chess was already firmly established in Western Europe and there are many references to it in literature. The game as played in the late 15th century had altered little in the preceding 500 years, but all at once a major change in the rules occurred, essentially transforming the game into the version we know today. The powers of the bishop and queen were vastly increased, and the pawn gained its initial double move. The effect was to increase the vitality of the game greatly; there was less slow manoeuvring and far more dynamic play. It has been suggested that this change was made to reflect new types of warfare, but it seems more likely that the main purpose was simply to improve the game. The 'new' chess rapidly caught on, and with minor modifications (such as the rules for castling) it has remained the same up to the present day.

Chess is now played worldwide, and over 140 countries participate in the biennial Chess Olympiads. In some countries of the Far East, what we call 'chess' is referred to as 'international chess' to distinguish it from local forms, such as Chinese chess. The popularity of the game is increasing and new developments, such as live games on the Internet, which make it possible to play in real time against opponents anywhere in the world, bode well for the future.

Chess must have some outstanding features to have captured people's imagination over a period of at least 1400 years. To see what these might be, one only has to look in the local computer games shop. The most popular computer games fall into two main categories: simulation and combat. In a simulation game, you might pilot a jet fighter or manage a football team, while combat games define themselves. Of course, these two categories may overlap to a greater or lesser extent, for example in a combat flight simulator. Nobody knows why chess was created, although colourful legends abound, but there can be little doubt that it was intended to be a simulation of warfare as it was conducted at the time. The aim of the game is the capture of the enemy king, the pawns (or peasants) lead the way into battle and are usually the first to disappear from the board, the knights can jump like a horse – the military analogies are too numerous to be coincidence. Lacking today's technology, the creators of chess based their simulation on a board game, something which, as we have seen, had already been popular for thousands of years and would be familiar to most people. It has been suggested that chess was originally used to train potential officers, but there seems to be no real evidence for this. In my view, it is unlikely; most of those who enjoy flight simulators have no intention of actually piloting a fighter, and if chess had been restricted to a military elite, then it would probably not have achieved such widespread popularity. Chess therefore combines both simulation and combat elements, but this in itself does not guarantee lasting success. Perhaps the key feature is that the level of difficulty is just right. Games that are too simple do not present enough of a challenge; no adult considers 3x3 tic-tac-toe a real game, since forcing a draw is incredibly simple. On the other hand, an overly complex game is unfulfilling, because nobody can master it. Chess falls somewhere in the middle; it has sufficient depth to be challenging, while at the same time it has peaks that can be scaled. The result is that anyone who spends time playing chess will notice a steady improvement in his (or her) ability. There will always be mysteries ahead – chess is a game that presents mysteries even for grandmasters – but equally there will be solid achievements and understanding. The 'one more game' appeal is similar to that of a video game, but it operates on a deeper level as it involves a gradual advance of knowledge and comprehension rather than the hand/eye coordination required to blast some aliens.

Chess has a reputation for being difficult to play. This is true in the sense that chess is a hard game to master, and even the world champion would admit that there is plenty of unexplored territory in chess. However, learning to play chess is not especially difficult and there is no reason why the beginner should not be enjoying his (or her) first games quickly. Perhaps the greatest difficulty in the early stages is finding a suitable opponent. As with most games and sports, contests between widely mismatched opponents usually lack interest. For more experienced players, there is a ranking system which makes it much easier to find an opponent of roughly one's own ability, but in the early days this is more difficult. I will return to this and other practical aspects of the game later in the book.

It must be admitted right away that the rules of chess do not fit on one page; part of the reason for this is that six different types of piece are involved, each moving in a different way. This is a consequence of the origin of chess as a simulation of warfare. Like all simulations, it is not completely straightforward – you would not expect to be able to sit down at a flight simulator and immediately perform a perfect landing. In compensation, once you have mastered the basic rules of chess you will be able to enjoy one of most enduring, challenging and exciting games ever invented.

It is interesting to note that most other popular 'mind games' also have rules which involve a certain complexity; for example, contract bridge has a fairly complex scoring system, while in go it's not that easy to say when the game has actually finished. There are very interesting and challenging games that have extremely simple rules, for example the childhood game of 'dots-and-boxes', but these games are often mathematically based and have not achieved the same popularity as games with 'real-world' origins.

2 The Rules of the Game

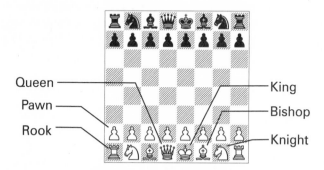

Queen — King
Pawn — Bishop
Rook — Knight

Basic Principles

The above diagram represents the starting position for every game of chess. I have named one piece of each type (the corresponding black pieces have the same names). Both players start with eight pawns, two rooks, two knights, two bishops, one queen and one king, positioned as indicated above. Normally, chess is played using three-dimensional wooden or plastic pieces. Although ornate chess sets are sometimes used for decorative purposes, chess sets used in competitive play adhere to a standard design called the Staunton pattern, after Howard Staunton (1810-74), one of the strongest players of his time. If you are going to buy a chess set, make sure that it is of the Staunton pattern, so that you become familiar with the design you will encounter at a chess club or in a tournament. You should have little difficulty matching up the pieces in a chess set with the symbols used in the diagram above. The only likely error is to confuse the king and the queen; however, knowing that the king always has a cross on top whilst the queen has a crown should solve that one.

If you are using computer software to look at chess positions on screen, then you should have even less trouble – in most cases the creators of software packages have modelled their screen designs on traditional printed chess diagrams such as that above. Some software has a '3-D' option, which offers a perspective view resembling what you would see during a tournament game. This is one of those things that you either love or hate. A '3-D' view is perhaps more realistic, but the board can appear confusing when there are many pieces close together, and quite often the pieces partially obscure one another. In a real game, you can move your head slightly to get a better view, but on screen it is not so easy. Personally, I prefer to be thinking about the position rather than trying to remember which key rotates the 3-D view about the z-axis.

Chess is a two-player game; when the two players are being described in generic terms, they are usually referred to as **White** and **Black**. Each player controls his own army of pieces. In the diagram on the previous page, the 16 pieces on the lower side of the diagram form White's army, while the 16 pieces at the top are Black's army. Chess diagrams are normally printed with White lower down the page. Most software packages have the option to 'Flip' or 'Invert' the board, so that Black is at the bottom. This is useful if, for example, you are Black and the computer is White. A couple of aspects of chess nomenclature sometimes cause confusion, so I will mention them straight away. The word 'White' can be used as a noun, when it is referring to one of the players. However, it can also be used as an adjective, as in 'the white rook is in the lower left corner of the board'. Here it is referring merely to the colour of the piece and is used without the initial capital letter. Note that, in chess writing, the pieces are always assumed to be coloured 'white' and 'black', even if in practice cream and dark brown pieces are quite common.

Finally, the board itself consists of 64 coloured squares and sometimes these are also referred to as 32 'white' and 32 'black' squares. In reality, the dark squares on a chessboard are rarely black, since the black pieces would then tend to merge into the squares. Dark green is the most common colour, while some shade of brown is not unusual. However, it is becoming accepted practice to use 'light' and 'dark' when referring to the squares on the board, a custom one can only applaud, as otherwise the words 'white' and 'black' are overloaded with different meanings. We will follow this convention and use 'light' and 'dark' for the squares on the board. When using software, the user can often modify the colours of the pieces and board at will, but it is not easy to find a combination that is pleasing to the eye. Some people may prefer a 1960s psychedelic chessboard, but I like white and black pieces, with light and dark brown squares.

The two players move alternately, with White moving first, until the game is finished. When it is your turn to move, you must do so; you cannot pass. You can only move pieces belonging to your own army; the only exception to this is when you capture an enemy piece, in which case you should remove the captured unit from the board. In practical play, once you have touched a piece, you have to move that piece if you can; this is called the **touch-move rule**. Once you have moved a piece to another square and released it, you can't change your mind and make a different move (even with the same piece). You may find that these rules are not always enforced in casual play, but you should get used to them as soon as possible because they are rigorously applied in club and tournament play. The discipline enforced by these rules is highly desirable in any case: you should only touch a piece when you are sure of the move you want to make.

The object of the game is the capture of the enemy king, yet, strangely enough, the rules state that the game is already over when the capture of the king is unavoidable next move. Thus the king is spared the humiliation of actually being removed from the board. The situation in which the king is under attack and will inevitably be captured next move is called **checkmate** or simply **mate** and it automatically ends the game. The player whose king faces unavoidable capture has lost the game. When starting out, you may find that it is not immediately obvious whether mate has occurred, but it will not be long before recognizing mate becomes second nature. The normal chess scoring system allocates one point for a win and zero points for a loss. A third result is possible, a **draw**, and in this case the two players receive half a point each. We shall see later that there are various ways in which the game can end in a draw.

The Moves of the Pieces

There are six different types of unit in chess: in order of decreasing value, these are king, queen, rook, bishop, knight and pawn. However, we will not tackle the pieces in this order. We will first deal with the three pieces that move in straight lines.

Line-Moving Pieces

The rook, bishop and queen all move in a similar way, by travelling as far as they like in a straight line, provided that their path is not blocked by another piece. These three pieces differ only in the direction of movement.

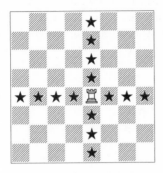 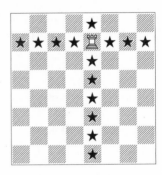

We shall use simplified diagrams such as the above when explaining the moves of the pieces; of course, in a position from a real game both kings and possibly other pieces would be present. The diagram on the left shows how a rook moves if there are no obstructions: vertically or horizontally, as far as the edge of the board. You don't have to go all the way to the edge; the rook can stop anywhere along the way. Thus in this position the rook can move to any of the 14 starred squares.

The right-hand diagram shows the situation after White has moved his rook three squares up the board. The stars again indicate those squares to which the rook could move if it were again White's turn to play; in a real game, of course, it would be Black's turn to play, and his move might change the situation.

On its new square, the rook again has 14 possible moves. It is a curious feature of the way the rook moves that it always has 14 possible moves, no matter which square the rook starts on, always providing that there is nothing in the way.

The rook, like the other line-moving pieces, the bishop and the queen, can be blocked by either friendly or enemy pieces.

The diagram overleaf shows how the rook can be obstructed by friendly pieces. To the left, one square is no longer available to the

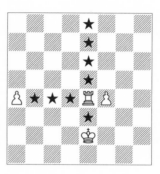

rook because it is already occupied by a white pawn. Downwards, the rook can still move one square, but the next square is occupied by White's own king so the rook cannot move there. This obstacle also prevents the rook moving to the square beyond. The rook, like the bishop and the queen, is not allowed to jump over pieces. A blocking pawn prevents any move by the rook to the right, so the rook only retains full freedom of movement upwards, where there is nothing in the way.

In the left-hand diagram, one of the friendly pawns has been replaced by an enemy pawn. The rook now has all the moves that were possible before, plus one extra. This extra move is the capture of the pawn to the left of the rook. Chess pieces capture by moving to a square currently occupied by an enemy piece. The right-hand diagram shows the result of White taking the enemy pawn with his rook. The rook now occupies the square where the pawn once stood, and the enemy pawn is removed from the board. With the exception of the pawn, all the chess pieces capture the same way that they move. By the way, you should never refer to the rook as a 'castle'; by using this incorrect name you will immediately identify yourself as a rank beginner (a similar *faux pas* is to call the knight a 'horse').

Although in one special case (pawn promotion – see page 32) a piece may be replaced by one of a different type, there is no mechanism in chess for captured pieces to reappear on the board (except for the start of the next game!). Thus the number of pieces on the board, which stands at 32 when the game starts, can only decrease as the game progresses. In the end there may only be a handful of pieces left on the board, but this does not mean the end of the struggle; on the contrary, these **endgame** positions have a special subtlety all their own, and we will return to them in Chapter 7.

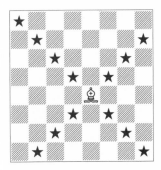 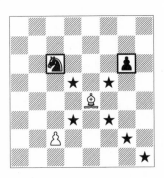

The bishop moves in a similar way to the rook, except that instead of moving laterally and vertically, it moves diagonally. The left-hand diagram above shows a bishop with 13 available moves. Unlike the rook, the number of squares available to an unobstructed bishop varies considerably according to the bishop's position. Thirteen is the maximum, but it can be as few as seven if the bishop occupies a square on the edge of the board. The right-hand diagram shows a bishop restricted by a variety of pieces. Just as with a rook, a piece that gets in the way also cuts off access to any of the squares beyond. This bishop has eight possible moves; the six non-capturing moves are starred, while either of the two black pieces may be captured by the bishop.

You may have already noticed one peculiarity in the way the bishop moves – if it stands on a light square, it can only move to another light square. This means that a bishop can only move to half the squares on the chessboard. If you look back to the initial position (see page 10), you will see that each player starts with two bishops, one standing on a light square and one on a dark square. Not surprisingly, these are referred to as a **light-squared bishop** and a **dark-squared bishop** respectively. These two bishops complement each other's actions, since together they can attack any square on the chessboard. If a player is forced to part with one bishop, say his dark-squared bishop, then his ability to attack dark squares will be reduced and he may have to make up the deficiency using his remaining pieces. The bishop is the only piece, apart from the pawn, which is restricted to just part of the board. All the other pieces have the ability to move to any square on the chessboard, given time and a cooperative opponent. On an open board, for example, a rook can reach any other square on the chessboard in at most two moves.

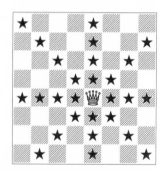 

The queen is the most mobile piece on the chessboard. You may recall that the reforms of the late 15th century increased the powers of the queen – and how! Before this time, the queen was a feeble piece but 500 years ago it was transformed into the most powerful unit on the board. The modern queen combines the powers of rook and bishop, and can move vertically, horizontally and diagonally. The left-hand diagram above shows the queen to its best advantage, able to move to 27 squares – almost half the board. The mobility of the queen, like that of the bishop, is affected by its position, but even on the edge of the board it is still capable of reaching 21 squares.

It might seem that such a powerful piece should be capable of delivering a quick knockout – like having an atomic bomb in your armoury. However, the fact that the queen is so powerful makes it very valuable; too valuable, in fact, to risk on uncertain ventures. If you dispatch your queen on mission impossible, then you may lose it and find yourself in the disastrous situation where your opponent has a queen but you do not. Beginners are often intoxicated by the power of the queen and make the error of sending it out on lone ventures. The queen *is* very powerful, but it usually needs the support of other pieces to be effective.

The right-hand diagram shows the queen operating when there are some other pieces on the board. The queen has 20 possible moves, including three moves that capture a black piece. Notice how the queen, because its action radiates along many 'spokes', is able to **attack several enemy pieces simultaneously**. This ability is of great practical importance and is one of the reasons why the queen is particularly valuable.

The mobility of any line-moving piece is affected by obstructions, so these pieces are at their best on an open board with few obstacles. Since most lines of activity pass through the central area of the board, any blocking pawns near the centre can profoundly affect the activity of your bishops, rooks and queen.

The Other Pieces

The three other pieces are the knight, pawn and king, each of which has its own individual characteristics.

The move of the knight is unique. It is the only chess piece that jumps directly from one square to another, non-adjacent, square. The left-hand diagram overleaf shows the eight moves that are available to a knight standing in the centre of the board. The knight's move takes a little getting used to, because it is less straightforward than the simple lateral or diagonal moves we have seen up to now. One way to look at it is that given in the right-hand diagram overleaf. To find the knight's possible destination squares, imagine it moving two

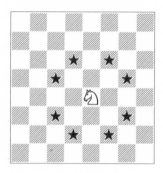 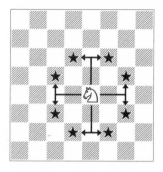

squares horizontally or vertically, and then turning to left or right through 90 degrees and moving one square further. There are four choices for the first leg, and each of these has two branches, so this gives the knight's eight possible destinations. It must be emphasized, however, that this way of looking at the knight's move is only to help work out the destination square. The knight does not actually slide along the board at all, but hops directly to its destination.

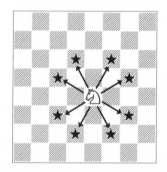 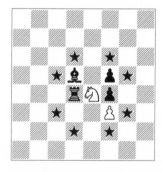

When you get used to the knight's move, you will think of it more as in the left-hand diagram above. This is perhaps a more accurate way to visualize the knight's move, which lies between the diagonal move of the bishop and the lateral move of the rook. If you were map-reading, you would call these directions NNW, NNE, ENE, and so on.

The jumping move of the knight means that it has properties quite unlike those of the other chess pieces. Take a look at the right-hand diagram above. How many moves does the knight have in this position? The answer is that it can still make the same eight moves as before. Because the knight jumps directly to its destination, **it cannot be blocked by intervening pieces**. Of course, if a friendly piece is standing on a potential destination square, then the knight cannot move there – you cannot have two pieces on the same square or capture your own pieces. Another feature of the knight's move is that **the colour of the square the knight stands on always changes** – the opposite of the bishop's behaviour. The odd move of the knight has paradoxical consequences. Look at the left-hand diagram below.

 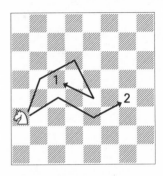

How many moves does it take the knight to reach the square marked '1'? How many to reach the square marked '2'? The surprising answer is that it takes a minimum of four moves to reach the first square, but only three to reach the second, even though the latter is much further away. The right-hand diagram shows possible routes (there are alternatives of equal length).

The knight differs from the line-moving pieces in that it is a short-range piece. If it is on one side of the board and it is suddenly needed on the other side, then it usually takes at least three moves to transfer the knight across. By the time the slow-moving knight arrives, it may well be too late to do any good. Consequently, handling the knight requires great care and anticipation.

The mobility of the knight is strongly affected by its position on the board, more so than with any other piece. Although it has eight possible moves when it stands in the centre of the board, this is reduced to four if it occupies a square in the middle of an edge, while a knight occupying a corner square has only two moves, just a quarter of its mobility in the centre. However, in one way the knight is a very effective piece. Like the queen, its influence extends along eight 'prongs', so it is capable of attacking a number of enemy pieces at once. Such a **knight fork** is very common in practice.

The pawn is, as its name suggests, the least powerful unit on the chessboard. But that is not to say that pawns are unimportant – on the contrary, handling pawns well is essential for success. At the start of the game half your army consists of pawns, and if they are not used to maximum advantage, you are throwing away one of your main assets. The pawn is unusual in that it is the only chess piece that captures in a different way to its normal move. First, let's look at the usual (non-capturing) move.

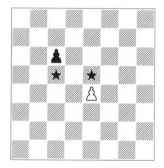 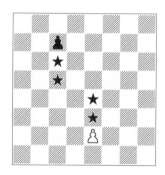

The left-hand diagram shows the normal move. Yes, that's all there is to it – one square forward. Not sideways, not diagonally and not backward – just forward. Black pawns move in a similar way, i.e. forwards from the point of view of a player sitting on Black's side of the board. The diagram also shows the possible move of a black pawn. The most obvious feature of the pawn's move is that it is irreversible – a pawn can't move backwards. For this reason grandmasters often take great care over pawn moves, because they know that if a pawn's advance should turn out to be mistaken, there is no way of correcting the error.

There is one exception to the one-step rule for a pawn. When a pawn makes its first move, it has the option of moving either one step or two steps forwards. The right-hand diagram shows the options available for a white pawn and black pawn standing on their original squares. The point of this rule is to make the game more dynamic; the initial double move allows the pieces standing behind the pawns to come into play more quickly. This is an example of the type of refinement one typically finds in games that have been around for a long time, and why these are generally more fun to play than modern 'invented' games. The initial double move of the pawn had been the subject of experimentation for at least 200 years before it was legitimized by the rule changes of the late 15th century. Only a few games have such a long history that players could agonize for a couple of centuries over a small change in the rules!

The left-hand diagram shows how the pawn captures; again one square forwards, but this time diagonally rather than straight ahead. Thus the pawn in the diagram can take either the black pawn or the black knight. The right-hand diagram shows the result if White decides to take the pawn. If it were Black to move in the left-hand diagram, then his pawn would be able to take the white pawn.

The double step on the pawn's initial move applies only to non-capturing moves. In the left-hand diagram overleaf, the white pawn has four possible moves: either to advance straight ahead to one of the starred squares, to take the black knight, or to take the black pawn. White cannot take the black bishop with his pawn.

The limited mobility of the pawn means that pawns often find themselves becoming stuck with no possible move. We speak of the

pawn as being **blockaded**. An especially common situation is when a white pawn and a black pawn face each other, as in the right-hand diagram above. The pawns blockade each other and at the moment neither can move. Later on the pawns might be freed; for example, if a black piece arrives on one of the starred squares, White might take it with his pawn, and then the black pawn would be free to advance.

Oddly enough, the importance of pawns lies largely in their limited movement and the ease with which they can be blockaded. The other pieces are able to move around the board at high speed, with the result that the situation on the board is changing moment by moment. The pawns, however, tend to stay in the same position for several moves (at least) and therefore provide the position with a more permanent structure – indeed, the formation of pawns on the board is often referred to as the **pawn-structure** or **pawn skeleton**. All long-term planning must take the pawn-structure into account, because this is one of the few features of the position that can usually be relied upon to remain constant. Equally, if for some reason the pawn-structure changes dramatically, then both players will have to review their plans in the light of the new situation. There is one more important point to mention about pawns, but we will deal with this later on (see 'Pawn promotion', page 32).

As is only fitting, we have left the king for last. In fact, the move of the king is perhaps the simplest of all the chessmen, but because capture of the king is the object of the game, some special points arise. The diagram on the next page shows how the king moves: one square in any direction – horizontally, vertically or diagonally. The king is

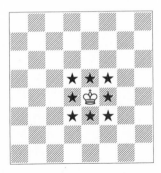

an even shorter-range piece than the knight; it takes a full seven moves for the king to cross the board from one edge to the opposite edge – an eternity in chess terms. Thus the position of the king is also a fairly long-term feature of the position. This is important in that the king is the primary target of the opponent's attack, so if it is moved to a vulnerable position, then the enemy attack may reach it before the error can be corrected.

We have already mentioned that the object of the game is capture of the enemy king, but the game actually ends just before this capture takes place, i.e. when the capture cannot be prevented from occurring next move. This goes hand in hand with an important rule that particularly affects king moves: **it is illegal to make a move that allows your king to be captured**. It follows that if capture of the king is unavoidable then you have no legal moves, which makes the rule about the end of the game appear more logical – having no legal moves implies a loss in many games besides chess.

However, it must be emphasized that the opposite of the above is not true; if you have no legal moves, it doesn't necessarily mean that you have lost the game. The crucial factor is whether your king is under attack or not.

In the left-hand diagram overleaf, Black to play has no legal moves. His only piece is his king, but all the squares the king might move to are covered by White's bishop or king. Thus Black has no legal moves, but his king is not under attack. This situation is called **stalemate**. If it arises, then the game immediately ends in a draw; in a tournament this would mean both players being awarded half a

point. One should not confuse the technical definition of stalemate in chess with the everyday use of the word. When one reads in a newspaper that 'negotiations are stalemated', it means that a situation of deadlock has arisen, which may be broken in the future. However, in chess it means that one player has no moves at all and represents the end of the conflict and not a halfway point. In the right-hand diagram above, the situation is similar to the left-hand diagram, but the difference is crucial. Black's king is under attack from White's knight, so this is not stalemate but checkmate, and Black has lost the game.

The rule that you cannot make a move which allows your king to be captured may severely restrict the number of king moves available, because it follows that you cannot move your king to a square controlled by an enemy piece.

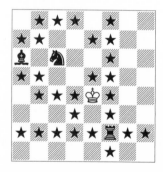

Take a look at the left-hand diagram. How many squares can White move his king to? The answer becomes clear in the right-hand diagram, in which the squares controlled by Black's pieces have been starred. Check that you understand which pieces are controlling the various starred squares. Of the potential maximum of eight squares, only two squares are actually available to the white king.

The fact that you cannot move your king to a square controlled by an enemy piece means, for example, that a position can never arise in which the white king stands next to the black king. The reason is that one player or the other must have moved his king to a square controlled by the enemy king, and this is not allowed.

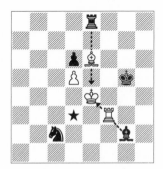 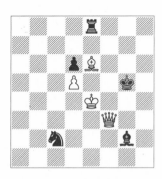

The rule about not putting your king under attack affects not only moves by the king. Take a look at the left-hand diagram above. How many legal moves does White have? The answer is that he has only one legal move (and is therefore forced to play it). This may appear surprising, since White has three pieces on the board in addition to his king. However, White cannot move his bishop as this exposes his king to attack by the black rook; by the same logic, he cannot move his rook as this would allow Black's bishop to take his king. White's pawn is blockaded and cannot move, which means White must move his king. The two squares to the right are covered by Black's king, one is covered by the black pawn while two more are covered by Black's knight. Thus White is forced to move his king to the starred square. White's bishop and rook are immobilized by Black's rook and bishop respectively; the lines of action are shown by the dotted arrows. Pieces that are paralysed like this (i.e. by the action of an enemy line-moving piece) are said to be **pinned**. This is a convenient moment to introduce a convention which will apply for the rest of the book. A **solid arrow** in a diagram indicates a move which is (or has been) actually played; a **dotted arrow** indicates a potential move or threat which may not actually occur.

In the superficially similar situation of the right-hand diagram, White has an extra move in addition to the king move he had earlier. The white queen, although pinned by the enemy bishop, nevertheless has a move: it can capture the black bishop.

There is one point that sometimes causes confusion. Can White move his knight in the above diagram? Certainly, moving the knight exposes White's king to attack by the enemy bishop. However, a lawyer might come along to confuse the issue by saying that Black could not actually take the white king with his bishop, as this would expose his own king to attack by White's rook! However, the common-sense rule is that White **cannot** move his knight in the above diagram. The obvious attack by the black bishop takes precedence over any tricky arguments. In other words, a piece can pin despite being pinned itself.

In the left-hand diagram at the top of the next page, Black has just moved his rook sideways until it is vertically above White's king. The rook is now attacking White's king and threatening to capture it. The situation in which a player threatens the enemy king is called **check**. Since it is illegal to allow the king to be captured next move, the player whose king is in check must respond to it by preventing the capture. In the left-hand diagram, White's only means of preventing the capture is to move his king out of the line of fire of Black's

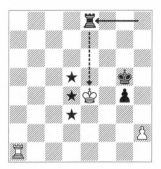 

rook. Since the squares to the right are controlled by Black's king and pawn, this means that White has to move his king to one of the three starred squares to the left. Checks occur quite often in chess – most games contain at least one.

In the diagram on the right, White is again in check, but this time there is no escape as Black's other rook is controlling the squares to the left of the white king. Since there is no way to prevent capture of the king next move, White has been mated and the game is over.

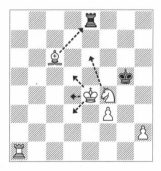 

In general, there are three possible ways to counter a check. The left-hand diagram demonstrates all three:

1) Move the king out of check. In this case, White has three king moves to the left which escape from the check.

2) Capture the checking piece. Here White can take the enemy rook with his bishop.

3) Interpose a piece between the checking unit and the king. This method only works if the check is from a line-moving piece. In the left-hand diagram, White can move his knight between the enemy rook and his king, thereby blocking the rook's attack. Incidentally, this move also checks the black king!

When they are checked, beginners often automatically touch their king and then look around for a place to move it, without first considering whether, for example, they can simply take the checking piece.

Now look at the right-hand diagram above. How many ways does White now have of escaping from the check? The answer is given after the next paragraph.

Checks are extremely important in chess. A check is a very forcing move; it compels the opponent to counter it immediately and gives him no time to continue with his own plans.

Now back to the right-hand diagram above. The answer is that now White has only three legal moves. He cannot take the checking rook with his bishop because the bishop is pinned – this capture would expose White's king to attack from the black queen in the corner. Likewise, he cannot interpose the knight because the knight is pinned by the rook to the right of it.

The Three 'Special' Moves

We are now not far away from finishing our coverage of the moves of the pieces. In fact, there remain only three exceptional moves which do not fit into the general pattern described above.

Of these, castling is the most important because it occurs in the vast majority of games. It is the only chess move in which two pieces move simultaneously; however, this double move is only allowed in one particular situation. Castling is a very useful move, as we shall see in due course. Since castling almost always occurs at an early stage of the game, we will take our examples from opening positions played in grandmaster games.

The left-hand diagram at the top of the following page features a common opening position. It is White to play, and while the position may appear confusingly crowded, we will focus on just two pieces: the white king and the rook to the right of it. Castling involves moving the king two squares towards the rook; the rook then hops over the king to land on the square immediately on the opposite side. The

arrows indicate these actions and the right-hand diagram shows the situation after the castling move has been completed.

Castling can also occur on the other side of the board. In the left-hand diagram, it is White to play and he is in a position to castle to the right, as seen in the previous diagram. However, he can also castle to the left. Just as before, the king moves two squares towards the rook and the rook then hops over the king to the square immediately beyond. Black might reply to this by castling himself; the right-hand diagram shows the situation after both sides have castled. The introduction of castling is the most recent major change to the rules of chess and was probably intended to speed up the game by allowing the players to develop their rooks more quickly.

Here is a little nomenclature to make our discussion of castling simpler.

The chessboard is often thought of as being divided into two halves, as labelled in the diagram above. The queenside is the half in which the queens start the game; the kingside is the half in which the kings start. While the initial position exhibits a fair degree of lateral symmetry, the single asymmetrical element – the position of the kings and queens – has a profound influence on the game. The distinction between queenside and kingside arises quite often, and this nomenclature is better than 'left' and 'right' because it does not depend on the side of the board one is looking from. The queenside is to White's left but Black's right, so the use of the terms 'queenside' and 'kingside' avoids a lot of confusion.

The two forms of castling are called **kingside castling** and **queenside castling**, according to the direction in which the king moves. Note that in both forms of castling, the king moves exactly two squares, and so the colour of the square on which the king stands remains unchanged. Castling is only legal when the following conditions are satisfied:

1) A king and a friendly rook stand on their original squares.

2) There are no pieces of either colour standing between the king and rook.

3) Neither king nor rook has moved so far during the game.

4) The king is not in check.

5) Neither the king's destination square nor the rook's destination square is attacked by an enemy piece.

One result of condition 3 is that you cannot state that castling is legal just by looking at the current position on the board; the previous course of the game is also relevant. You might see the king and the rook on their original squares, but you can never know whether one of them might have moved and then returned to its original square later on.

Condition 4 is usually summarized by the phrase 'you cannot castle out of check'. Here are a couple of positions to test your grasp of the castling rules:

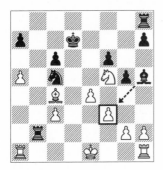 

The left-hand diagram is from a game played between Ivkov and Rukavina in the 1975 Yugoslav Championship held in Novi Sad. White is to move and neither his king nor his rooks have so far been moved. Can he castle kingside? Can he castle queenside?

The answer to both questions is yes. There is no reason at all why he should not castle kingside. Castling queenside is also legal. It is true that the nearby black rook controls a square the rook must jump over, but this is no impediment to castling. Referring back to rule 5 above shows that this square does not matter. Note, however, that the white pawn on the highlighted square is important. If it were not for this pawn, the square that White's rook ends up on would be covered by Black's bishop, and then queenside castling would not be legal. White did in fact castle queenside (*see the right-hand diagram*), which was such a strong move that Black immediately surrendered, or **resigned**, as it is normally put in chess. The point is that both the pieces involved in the queenside castling have suddenly moved to damaging positions. The rook checks the black king, forcing Black to respond; meanwhile, the king attacks the nearby black rook. However Black answers the check, White is able to take the rook with his king next move. In a game between players of national championship level, the advantage of an extra rook is so great that Black saw no point in continuing the struggle.

In practice, kingside castling is considerably more common than queenside castling because the latter requires three intervening pieces to be moved out of the way beforehand, while the former only requires two. Thus kingside castling can usually be achieved with the expenditure of less time and effort than queenside castling.

Now we move on to the second 'special' move: pawn promotion. Pawns may be the weakest units on the chessboard, but they possess a unique power – the ability to change into another piece. This rule is quite simple: if a pawn reaches the opposite side of the board, then, as part of the same move, the pawn must be removed from the board and replaced by a knight, bishop, rook or queen of the same colour.

The diagrams above show how pawn promotion works. White advances his pawn by the normal pawn move to the far side of the board, removes the pawn and replaces it with a piece of his choice, in this case the queen. As we shall see on page 70, a position with king and queen against king is winning, so White's pawn promotion has effectively decided the game.

There are several points to note about pawn promotion:

1) All the actions involved take place as part of the same move.

2) When the pawn makes the last step to the other side of the board, the promotion is not optional: you must immediately decide which piece you want to promote to, and replace the pawn with that piece.

3) Given the choice of rook, bishop, knight or queen, it is most natural to choose the queen, since this is the most powerful piece available. In real-life games, the queen is chosen more than 99% of the time, but there are a few special situations in which it is better to choose one of the lesser pieces (this is called **underpromotion**). See page 49 for an example of this situation.

4) Once the promotion has taken place, the newly-created piece has exactly the same powers as if it had been on the board the whole time.

5) Even if you still have your original queen, there is nothing to stop you promoting a pawn to a second queen (the same applies to any other choice of promoted piece). Theoretically, you could even end up with nine queens on the board if you promoted all your pawns. If you promote a pawn to a second queen, there is the practical difficulty of finding another queen to put on the board. This is not normally a problem at a chess club or tournament, where you can usually find an unused queen on another board to confiscate. However, in friendly games played at home it can cause more of a problem, so there is a convention that if a second queen is not available then you can use an upturned rook to represent the queen. Of course, if neither rook has been captured (or if you end up with nine queens!) then you still have a problem, but such a situation is extremely rare.

The promoting pawn move can also be a capture. The above pair of diagrams shows how devastating such a move can be. The white pawn takes the black queen, at the same time promoting to a queen.

Thus Black goes two queens down in one move! After such a catastrophe, it hardly seems worth mentioning that the move also gives checkmate. The black king is in check from both white queens at the same time and has no way to escape. Note that the king cannot capture the newly-created queen as it is defended by the white bishop. A situation in which a king is in check from two pieces at the same time is called **double check**. Double checks are particularly dangerous because of the three methods of escaping from a check (running away, capturing the checking piece and blocking), only one (running away) is available.

Pawn promotion is a very important possibility in chess. It is true that it does not often occur in grandmaster games, but this is only because one player usually resigns before promotion can occur. If all games were played out to mate, then pawn promotion would occur in the majority of them. When grandmasters play each other, they agonize about the possible loss of a pawn, and often go to great lengths to win one. Why? It is not so much that the extra pawn is especially useful in itself, but as the game progresses and the pieces gradually disappear from the board, there is less and less to prevent the extra pawn advancing to the other side of the board to become a queen. With an extra queen, the win is easy. Without pawn promotion, the advantage of a single pawn would not be especially significant; as it is, an extra pawn without any compensation leads to a win more often than not.

The final 'special move' goes by the French name of '*en passant*' or, 'the *en passant* capture'. It can occur only in one special situation.

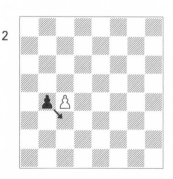

The sequence of diagrams above (labelled 1-3) shows how the *en passant* capture works. In Diagram 1, White is about to move his pawn. If he advances it one square, then Black can take it with his own pawn in the normal way. However, White instead makes the double advance, which is allowed when the pawn stands on its original square. Diagram 2 shows the position after White's move. The *en passant* rule allows Black to take the white pawn even after the double move. The capture is made exactly as if the white pawn had only advanced one square. The black pawn moves one square diagonally, and the white pawn disappears from the board. The final situation is shown in Diagram 3. Diagram 4 shows how the rule applies in a similar way when a black pawn is captured.

Some points about the *en passant* capture:

1) It only applies to the capture of one pawn by another pawn.

2) The option to make the *en passant* capture only exists for one move. If you do not take it up straight away, then it disappears.

3) You usually cannot tell if *en passant* is possible just by looking at the board, without any knowledge of the history of the game (a similar situation arises with respect to castling), because you do not know the last move played.

Starting and Finishing a Game

Starting a game is easy enough. You just set up the board and pieces as in the diagram on page 10, White plays the first move and the game is under way. However, it is important to arrange the board and pieces correctly. One of the most common errors is to start with the board the wrong way round. The basic rule here is that whichever side of the board you are sitting on, the corner square near you on the right-hand side should be a light square. It is curious that, although chess sets are often used in advertising, they seem to be the wrong way round more than 50% of the time!

The other error which occurs from time to time is to transpose the king and queen. The white queen should always be placed on a light square and the black queen on a dark square. The two kings should face each other across the board; likewise the two queens.

In competitive games, the players are assigned White and Black before the game by the tournament controller (the precise rules for this vary widely from event to event). This can be an important matter, as White, moving first, normally holds a slight advantage. Between grandmasters, White scores roughly 55% to Black's 45%. However, at lower levels the difference between White and Black is much less significant, because considerable skill is required to make anything of the slight advantage of moving first. In casual games, colours are normally drawn by lot. The traditional method of doing this is for one player to shake a white pawn and a black pawn together and then hold out two fists, each concealing a pawn. The other player then chooses one and starts with the colour of the pawn thus revealed. If you have not seen this ritual before, it probably looks rather odd, but it does seem to be virtually universal. It is also worth mentioning that in competitive games it is customary for the two players to shake hands before the game and at its conclusion.

There is much more variety in the way a game can end. Dealing with decisive results first, delivering mate is the most straightforward way for the game to end. When you are starting out, this is probably the way most games will end. Amongst more experienced players, resignation in a hopeless position is the most common conclusion. Traditionally, resignation is acknowledged by tipping over one's own king, but in serious tournament play stopping the **chess clocks** (see page 186) is also very common. Deciding when to resign is an art in itself, and chess history is full of instances in which a player resigned, only to discover afterwards that the position was not lost at all. The only real guidance I can offer is only to resign if you are **really sure** that your position is hopeless. More experienced players are sometimes exasperated when their time is 'wasted' by someone playing on against them in a hopeless position, but it is your right to play on if you want to. In tournament play with chess clocks, it is also possible to lose by exceeding your time allocation, but we will deal with such matters in Chapter 10.

The game can also end in a draw in a variety of ways. We have already mentioned stalemate (see page 23), but there are other possibilities. Some of these are only really relevant to tournament play, but we mention them here in order to complete our coverage of the rules.

The simplest way the game can end in a draw is for the two players simply to agree to a draw. If it is your turn to move, then you can, at the same time as making your move, offer a draw. This is normally done by either the formal "I offer a draw" or the less formal "Would you like a draw?". The opponent can then either accept the draw, reject it verbally (usually by saying "I would like to play on") or make a move, thereby rejecting it by implication. Some players consider the last of these possibilities impolite, so if you want to reject a draw offer it is probably best to do so verbally. Once you have offered a draw, you cannot withdraw the offer. However, if your opponent rejects it (either verbally or by making a move) then the draw offer is nullified; he cannot then change his mind and accept it later. There is a certain etiquette to making draw offers. Obviously, you should only do so if the position is genuinely equal; offering a draw in a position where you have a manifest disadvantage only serves to irritate the opponent. Also, you should not pester your opponent with draw offers. If he has rejected one offer, it is better to wait for him to make the next offer, if he wants to.

It should be emphasized that the facility for the players to agree a draw is really only intended to be used when all possibilities to play for a win have been exhausted. In this case, a position may arise which is so completely equal that neither player can reasonably hope to win. However, one's perception of when the winning chances are exhausted depends very much on one's playing strength. A game between two grandmasters may be agreed drawn in a position that would appear to offer interesting play to someone of lower playing strength. In tournaments, it may also happen that a draw is agreed for reasons which have nothing to do with the position on the board; for example, a draw may guarantee one player first place and his opponent second place. Rather than risk their standings, the players may prefer to agree a quick draw rather than fight it out. On the whole, I think it is better to avoid offering draws until your playing strength is relatively high (club player, at least). Your judgement on whether you have the advantage or not is likely to be uncertain, and you may be throwing away possible wins by agreeing premature draws. Also, at this stage your main ambition should be to learn more, and little is learnt by agreeing to an early draw. However, the detailed description of the process given above should help you in case your opponent offers you a draw.

The game can also end in a draw if the same position arises three times, with the same player to move and the same possibilities to move on the board. This last condition is a rarely-invoked technical detail stating that the two players must have the same castling and *en passant* possibilities, otherwise the repetition does not count. If there is such a **threefold repetition**, a draw can be claimed (although this is not compulsory). The precise rules for claiming such a draw are quite complex, and are only relevant for tournament play where the players have kept a record of the game for the arbiter to check the claimed repetition. We will not go into these details, because you are only likely to encounter one situation that gives rise to a repetition of position: **perpetual check**.

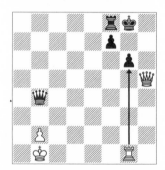 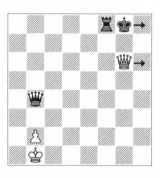

The above diagrams show a typical example. White is to play in the left-hand diagram. He is a pawn down, and if the game were to continue quietly, then he might well lose in the long run. He therefore decides to sacrifice his rook. The arrow shows the move he plays, taking Black's pawn with his rook. Black is forced to take the rook with his pawn, and White then makes a second capture on the same square with his queen. The position arising is shown in the right-hand diagram. Black is in check, and has only one possible move to escape the check, shifting his king to the right. However, White can match this move by also moving his queen to the right one square, again delivering check. Black's only possible response is to return with his king; White does the same with his queen, and the position is repeated. This is a typical perpetual check. In practice, the players, seeing this familiar pattern in front of them, would agree a draw straight away and not wait for the threefold repetition to be completed. Perpetual check arises relatively often in practice, and it can offer a saving resource to a player who would otherwise lose.

Another drawing possibility is that of **insufficient material**. It is impossible to win with king against king, king and bishop against king, king and bishop against king and bishop (with the bishops moving on same-coloured squares) or king and knight against king (in all cases assuming there is no other material on the board). No mating positions are possible with these material balances, so you cannot win, even with your opponent's cooperation. In these cases a draw should be declared immediately. This is a very obscure rule, included here only for the sake of completeness, and in all my years of tournament play I have never seen it invoked.

The final drawing possibility is the **fifty-move rule**. I mentioned earlier that the game is often agreed drawn if the winning possibilities have been exhausted and the players are reduced to shuffling around aimlessly. The fifty-move rule is designed to cater for obstinate opponents who will not agree to a draw in such a situation. It states that if fifty consecutive moves have been made by both players, with no capture or pawn move having been made in this period, then it is possible for one player to claim a draw. As with the three-fold-repetition rule, the precise details of claiming the draw are only relevant for tournament play. The use of this rule is extremely rare; in all my thousands of tournament games played during a career spanning over 30 years, I have never had to invoke the 50-move rule.

Computer playing programs, such as the strong and popular *Fritz* (now on version 12), are stronger than any human opponent if run on a powerful PC, so it might seem that they would not be very useful for beginners. However, such programs have a number of features which can be helpful when learning to play chess. If you are choosing a piece of chess software, you should check which beginner-friendly features it supports. Obviously, all programs should prevent you from entering an illegal move, but some go much further. I will use *Fritz* as an example of the type of features you might find in a chess software package. All the features I will discuss are optional, and you can turn them off when you no longer need them. One of the most useful features is also the simplest: when you click on one of your own pieces, *Fritz* can indicate the legal moves available for that piece. This is certainly a help in becoming familiar with the moves of the pieces. The various moves are also colour-coded, so that you see if your intended move allows the immediate capture of the piece. *Fritz* can also indicate which of your own pieces are under threat, so that you don't overlook a sneaky threat by *Fritz*. Taking moves back isn't allowed in competitive chess, but you can do it against *Fritz* without eliciting even a beep of protest.

There are also 'Coach' and 'Explain all' facilities. The 'Coach' is sometimes quite useful in pointing out if you have overlooked something important. 'Explain all' lists all the legal moves available to you in a given position and appends a brief comment to each one. However, computer programs gain their playing strength by the high-speed examination of a large number of positions; they don't understand chess in the same way as a human being. Consequently, the computer's attempts to explain moves in human terms often fall rather flat; many moves are described as 'OK', 'playable' or 'not wrong', which isn't especially helpful. While computer software offers many features which are helpful to the beginner, it is important not to become dependant on these aids. When you are facing a human opponent across the board, there won't be any flashing squares or little arrows to indicate your opponent's threats; if you make a mistake, the only visual indication that something is amiss will be the smug grin on your opponent's face as he snaps off your undefended piece. You can adjust the playing strength of *Fritz* – just as well, as playing *Fritz* at full power is only likely to be depressing. In one mode, *Fritz* attempts to adjust its playing strength to your own, and you can add a handicap factor so that either you or the machine has an edge.

There are also software packages specifically geared to beginners. One of the most popular is the *Fritz and Chesster* series, which is aimed at kids. The first disc teaches how the pieces move based on a series of mini-games, while the later discs (there are currently three altogether in English) move on to mates and tactics.

Despite the advantages of using a computer, not the least of them being that you keep your embarrassing blunders to yourself (until someone develops a virus which transmits your blunders all over the Internet, that is), there is no doubt that it is more fun to confront a human opponent. The practical questions of finding suitable opponents, playing on the Internet, and so on, will be dealt with in a later chapter.

Exercises

1) The players have set up the board for the start of the game, but they have made two mistakes. What are they?

2) How many possible moves can White make with his rook? If the white pawn is replaced by a black rook, how many can White now make?

3) How many possible moves can White make with his bishop? If the bishop is moved to the starred square, how many can White make now? In the latter case, how many of these moves check the black king?

5) How many possible moves can White make with his knight? How many are captures? How many knight moves check the black king? Are any of these mate?

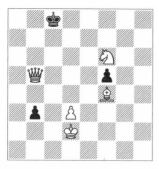

4) How many moves can White make with his queen? How many of these are captures? How many queen moves check the black king? How many of these checks are mate?

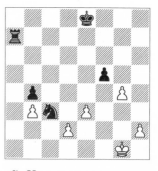

6) How many pawn moves can White make? How many of these are captures? If the black rook is replaced by a black bishop, how many pawn moves can White then make?

7) How many king moves can White make? If the black knight is replaced by a black rook, how many can White then make?

9) White is to play. Find a move that mates Black. Now find an alternative move that stalemates Black.

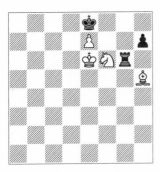

8) Is this checkmate?

10) White is to play. Can he mate immediately? Suppose the black pawn is removed. Can White still mate immediately?

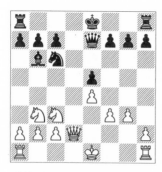

11) Assume the kings and rooks have never moved. White is to play. Can he castle kingside? What about queenside? If it were Black to play, which side or sides would he be able to castle?

13) Black, to play, advances his pawn two squares. Can White take it *en passant*? Is your answer the same if the black knight is replaced by a black rook?

12) How many ways can White promote his pawn (counting promotion to queen, rook, etc. as different moves)? Is it possible to mate Black with one of these pawn promotions? Now suppose that Black's rook is moved two squares to the left. Answer the same questions in this case.

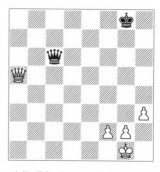

14) Black, to play, is three pawns down, a material disadvantage which is almost always fatal. However, in this position, Black can save the game. How?

15) Can you ever have two bishops, both operating on the light-coloured squares?

16) Is it possible to deliver mate with a king move?

17) Suppose you are in check. Is it ever possible to deliver mate without capturing the checking piece?

18) Is it possible to give double check with a king move?

19) Is it possible to give double check with a pawn move?

Solutions to Exercises

1) The first mistake is that the black king and queen have been swapped. Remember that the black queen starts on a dark square. The second mistake is that White's bishop and knight have been transposed on the left-hand side of the board.

2)

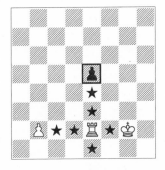 

The left-hand diagram shows the seven possible moves by the white rook (including the capture of the black pawn). In the right-hand diagram, White cannot move his rook vertically, as this would expose his own king to attack from the black rook. However, one extra move has been introduced: White can now capture the black rook, giving a total of four possible moves.

3)

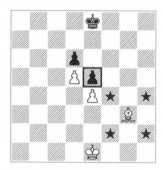 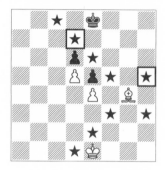

The solution to the first part is easy enough. The left-hand diagram shows the bishop's five possible moves, one involving the capture of a black pawn.

Moving the bishop one square up the board gives us the right-hand diagram. There are now nine squares for the bishop. If it moves to one of the two highlighted squares, the bishop checks Black's king.

4)

 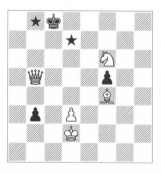

The white queen has 16 possible moves, which are shown in the left-hand diagram. Two of these are captures (highlighted in the diagram). Nine are checks. Two queen moves mate the black king; these are indicated by stars in the right-hand diagram.

5)

White can make seven moves with his knight, as shown in the left-hand diagram. One is a capture (highlighted in the diagram). Two knight moves check the black king (indicated by stars in the right-hand diagram). The move to the upper right (highlighted) mates Black. The other possible check is not mate as it blocks the white rook and allows the black king to run away.

6)

White can make eight possible pawn moves (indicated by arrows in the left-hand diagram). Two of these are captures. If the black rook is replaced by a black bishop, then White can only make seven pawn moves. This is because the highlighted pawn is pinned by the black bishop and cannot move without exposing White's king to check.

7)

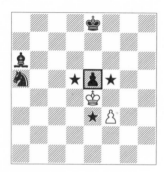 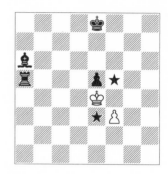

The left-hand diagram shows the four possible king moves (including the capture of Black's pawn). When the knight is replaced by a rook, there are only two possible moves, as shown in the right-hand diagram.

8) Yes, it is checkmate. White's knight is attacking Black's king, and the king can't run away as the white king and pawn cover all the possible escape-routes. Finally, Black cannot take the knight with his rook, as this would expose his king to the attack of White's bishop.

9)

The left-hand diagram shows how White can mate. The right-hand diagram shows how White can stalemate.

10)

The left-hand diagram shows how White can mate. If the black pawn is removed, then the knight move no longer mates, because the black king can move to the square formerly occupied by the pawn. However, removing the pawn opens the h-file and allows an entirely different mate by the white queen, which is shown in the right-hand diagram.

11) White cannot castle kingside, because the square his king would end up on is attacked by Black's bishop. White can, however, castle queenside. If it were Black to play, he could not castle queenside as the square his rook ends up on would be attacked by the white queen. Black could, however, castle kingside.

12)

There are eight different ways White can promote his pawn. He can push it straight ahead, or he can take Black's rook. In each of these two cases, White can choose between queen, rook, bishop or knight, to give a total of eight. Only one of these eight possibilities mates Black (shown in the left-hand diagram). This is one of the rare cases where it is better not to choose a queen when promoting a pawn.

In the second case, there are again eight possible promotions. Only one gives mate and this time White must promote to a queen to achieve his aim, as shown in the right-hand diagram.

13) Yes, White can take the pawn *en passant*. However, when the black knight is replaced by a black rook, the *en passant* capture is no longer possible. The reason is that it removes both pawns from the line joining the black rook and the white king, and therefore exposes White's king to capture.

14)

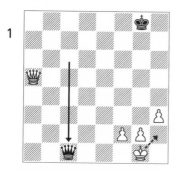

Black's drawing idea is a standard ploy, but it seems almost miraculous the first time you see it. Black starts with a queen check, as in Diagram 1. If White does not want to give his queen away, the reply is forced – White must move his king away from the attack of Black's queen. Black again gives a queen check, as in Diagram 2. If White again moves his king, then Black returns with his queen to its previous square, checking again – perpetual check. The only way for White to avoid this is to push his pawn, as indicated by the arrow. Then, however, Black can take a pawn with check, as in Diagram 3.

White's reply is forced, but Black continues checking with his queen (see Diagram 4) – perpetual check again. White's king cannot avoid the attentions of Black's queen, and the game is a draw.

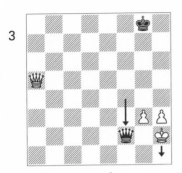

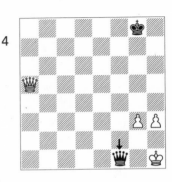

15) Yes, you can. If one of your pawns reaches the other side of the board, then you can promote it to a bishop. If this should occur on a light square, and you still have your original light-squared bishop, then you have two light-squared bishops on the board at the same time. I should add that, although this is possible, it is incredibly rare.

16) Yes, this is possible. A king cannot give check directly, but it can uncover a check from another piece.

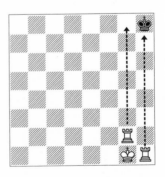

The above diagrams show one possibility. White's king slips out of the way of the rook, uncovering a check onto Black's king. A check such as this, in which one piece opens up a line for the checking piece, is called a **discovered check**. In this case it is even mate, as the rooks work together to deny Black's king any refuge.

17) Yes, this is possible and there are several ways it might occur.

 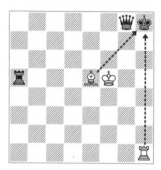

The left-hand diagram is an example. White's king is in check from Black's rook. The reply not only blocks the check, but also puts Black's king in double check. The only possible answer to a double check is a king move, but here no king moves are available.

18) No, it is impossible to give double check with a king move.

19) Yes, this is possible in several different ways.

The above diagrams show one possibility involving a pawn capture. It is also possible to give double check by a pawn promotion.

3 Chess Notation

Up to now, we have displayed moves using a system of diagrams and arrows. This has the defect of consuming a great deal of space; two moves by both sides occupy the best part of a page. Long ago, various systems of writing down chess moves in a compact form were devised. From these, the **algebraic system** has emerged as a *de facto* worldwide standard. Although there are some minor variations in the details, this method is now universally accepted. I should mention that if you look at some old English-language books, you may find an alternative system, the so-called 'descriptive system', but this has now fallen into disuse and I will not describe it.

The word 'algebraic' probably invokes memories of school mathematics, but with regard to chess notation, the word simply implies that a system of coordinates is used.

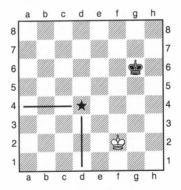

This diagram shows how the coordinates are applied to a chessboard. Starting from the bottom-left corner, the letters 'a' to 'h' are applied across the bottom of the board, while the numbers '1' to '8' run up the left-hand edge. For the sake of convenience, we have repeated these letters and numbers on the other two edges of the board. The lines show how it works: the starred square is directly above the 'd' and directly to the right of the '4', so we say that this square is 'd4'. Each of the 64 squares is given a unique name in the same way, from 'a1' in the bottom left corner to 'h8' in the top right corner. This system will be utterly familiar to anyone who has ever used a map, which I suppose will be almost everybody.

You should be able to verify that the white king stands on f2 and the black king on g6. You will often find comments in chess books such as 'White must attack the g6-pawn'. The phrase 'the g6-pawn' is a shorthand for 'the pawn standing on the g6-square'.

Now that we have named the squares, how do we actually write down a move?

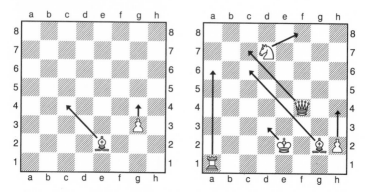

Suppose White moves his bishop as indicated by the arrow in the left-hand diagram. You can see that the bishop starts on e2 and ends up on c4. We therefore write this move as '♗e2-c4', meaning 'the bishop moves from e2 to c4'. The small **figurine** is a miniature version of the symbol used for the bishop in chess diagrams. Moves by the other pieces use similar figurines (the complete list is ♔=king, ♕=queen, ♖=rook, ♗=bishop, ♘=knight). No figurine is used for pawn moves, so the pawn move in the left-hand diagram is written g3-g4. Have a look at the moves in the right-hand diagram. They are written ♖a1-a6, ♘d7-f8, ♔e2-d3, ♕f4-c7, ♗g2-c6 and h2-h4.

These days, the use of figurines is quite common in both books and magazines, but it is by no means universal. The alternative is to use letters to represent the pieces; this has the defect that the letters employed vary from language to language. The standard letters in English are K for king, Q for queen, R for rook, B for bishop and N for knight. The use of 'N' for knight is a necessary compromise, as the obvious 'K' has already been used for the king. When recording games by hand (this is compulsory in competitive chess) it is normal to use the letters; drawing the figurines would be rather time-consuming, although I know of at least one grandmaster who does this! Even if you are faced with a foreign-language publication that doesn't use figurines, it won't take you long to learn the letters used for pieces. In German, for example, they are K for king, D for queen, T for rook, L for bishop and S for knight. Thanks to the universal system of chess notation, it is easy to play over games in books published in virtually any language.

The remaining features of chess notation are really just icing on the cake. If a move is a capture, then the symbol 'x' is used instead of '-'. If a move delivers check, then a '+' is appended to the move. Sometimes you will find '++' used for a double check and '#' used to indicate checkmate, but these two symbols are not absolutely standard. However, we will use them in this book.

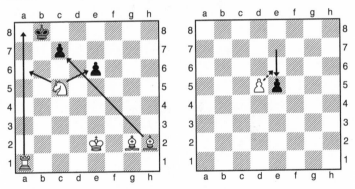

The left-hand diagram provides some examples of these symbols: ♖a1-a8#, ♘c5-a6+, ♘c5xe6, ♗h2xc7+.

A few last points concerning the three 'special' moves: castling kingside is written '0-0' and castling queenside is written '0-0-0'. Black moves are preceded by '...'. When a pawn promotes, it is necessary to give the piece promoted to as well as the start and destination squares: a typical example is e7-e8♕, indicating that the pawn is promoted to a queen. Finally, the right-hand diagram shows an *en passant* capture. Black has just played ...e7-e5 and White will now take the pawn by playing his own pawn to e6 and removing the e5-pawn from the board. Is this written d5xe5 or d5xe6? The answer is d5xe6: it is the starting and finishing squares of the moving piece that count.

Now it is time for you to practice your grasp of chess notation by playing over our first complete game. If you have a chess set or some chess software now is the time to get it out (or start it up). Try to play over the following game. I will provide a diagram every few moves so that you can check that you are on track.

M. Al Modiahki – Tin Htun Zaw
Yangon (Myanmar) 1999

1	e2-e4	g7-g6
2	d2-d4	♗f8-g7

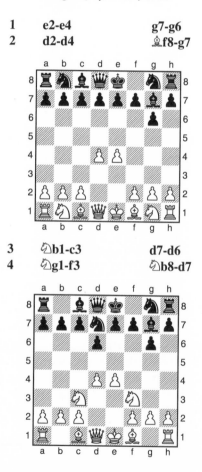

3	♘b1-c3	d7-d6
4	♘g1-f3	♘b8-d7

5	♗f1-c4	c7-c5
6	♘f3-g5	♘g8-h6
7	♗c4xf7+	♘h6xf7

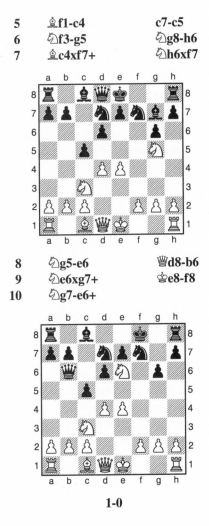

8	♘g5-e6	♛d8-b6
9	♘e6xg7+	♚e8-f8
10	♘g7-e6+	

1-0

First of all, what's all that stuff at the beginning of the game? When quoting a game, it is usual to give the names of the players, where and in which year the game was played, and sometimes the opening. We won't mention the opening, because we have not yet talked about opening play, but the names of the players and the venue are given. Al Modiahki is a grandmaster from Qatar, while Tin Htun

Zaw is a highly-ranked player from Myanmar (formerly Burma). The first-named player is always White. The game was played in an international tournament held in Yangon (formerly Rangoon), the capital of Myanmar. Moves in a chess game are generally numbered, with one white move and one black move counting as one 'move' for numbering purposes. These are the numbers given in the left-hand column. The second column contains White's moves, while the third column contains Black's moves. Thus White began with e2-e4, Black replied ...g7-g6, White played d2-d4 and so on. Often, in order to save space, the moves are not given in columns but are just run on; for example, 1 e2-e4 g7-g6 2 d2-d4 ♗f8-g7, etc. Finally, what about the '1-0' at the end? This is a standard languageless shorthand for 'White wins'; in a similar way '0-1' means 'Black wins' and '½-½' represents a draw.

We will return to this game later to see how White managed to win so quickly and where Black went wrong. In chess publications, you will often see moves adorned with exclamation marks and question marks. Doubtless you will have already guessed that this is another shorthand. The exclamation marks and question marks are not part of the game itself, but are a form of commentary. If you see 7 ♗c4xf7+!, for example, this means that somebody thought that taking on f7 was a good move, while in a similar way '!!' means a brilliant move, '?' means a bad move and '??' means a blunder. Normally the author of these comments, or **annotator**, is named somewhere, although (especially in magazines) it is sometimes not clear from whom they originate. I should emphasize that these symbols are only used when reproducing games in publications and they should not be used when you are recording a game in a tournament. If your opponent plays a move, you write it down and then add '??' to it, your opponent will almost certainly take offence! There are two other commonly accepted symbols which it is worth mentioning: '?!' means a dubious or doubtful move – not as serious as a 'bad' move, but still not to be recommended. Finally, '!?' means an 'interesting' move – this is the vaguest of the common symbols, and can mean anything from 'risky but may succeed in practice' to 'I haven't a clue about this move'.

We have introduced quite a lot of symbols, so here is a table summarizing them:

0-0	castles kingside
0-0-0	castles queenside
+	check
++	double check
#	checkmate
x	capture
!!	brilliant move
!	good move
!?	interesting move
?!	dubious move
?	bad move
??	blunder
1-0	the game ends in a win for White
½-½	the game ends in a draw
0-1	the game ends in a win for Black

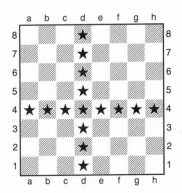

Some lines of squares on the chessboard are given special names. The vertical lines of squares stretching from the bottom of the board to the top are called **files**. In the diagram above, all the squares on the **d-file** are starred. There are eight files, running from the a-file on the left side to the h-file at the far right.

Similarly, the horizontal lines of squares are called **ranks**. In the diagram above, all the squares along the **fourth rank** have been starred. There are eight ranks, running from the first rank at the bottom of the board to the eighth rank at the top. There is some ambiguity in the naming of ranks. Most often, the absolute numbering given above is used. However, sometimes you will see a phrase such as **Black's first rank**, that is to say the rank nearest Black, which is the eighth rank from White's point of view. Another way of looking at the co-ordinate system is to say that the square d4 lies at the intersection of the d-file and the fourth rank. The diagonals are not normally given special names, except for the **long diagonals**, which run from a1 to h8 and from h1 to a8.

Perhaps I should come clean at this stage and admit that the form of chess notation described above, called **long algebraic**, is not the most common in chess literature. However, it is the most suitable for beginners and you will find it used in many elementary textbooks. The alternative, and more common, form is called **short algebraic** and is very similar to the long form except that only the destination square of the piece is mentioned. Once again, the motivation is to save space. In the short form, the above game would start 1 e4 g6 2 d4 ♗g7 3 ♘c3, etc. This is more complex for the reader because when you see '♘c3', for example, you have to locate c3, and then look to see which knight can reach c3 in one move. The long form is simpler since '♘b1-c3' tells you immediately that you should look on b1. The short form also has to cope with the situation in which, for example, two rooks can move to the same square. When you have been using the long form for some time, you should have little trouble switching to the short form. However, it is worth noting that even some grandmasters prefer to record their games in long algebraic, perhaps because they find it intrinsically clearer.

If you are using computer software, the computer will typically display the current position on a graphical representation of a chessboard, while displaying the moves of the game in algebraic notation. You should be able to switch between the long and short forms of algebraic notation (the popular *Fritz* program mentioned earlier can do this, for example). At one time you had to enter moves by typing in the notation, but these days it is much easier to play the move on the graphical board with the mouse.

Chess is fortunate that games are so easy to record. When all these space-saving shortcuts are used, a game of chess takes up very little space on the printed page and so publications can contain hundreds or even thousands of games. The literature of chess is vast. Arab manuscripts existed 1,000 years ago, and the invention of the printing press in the mid-15th century was put to use for practical chess books before that century had come to an end. Since then the total number of books has increased dramatically and it is hard to give even a rough estimate for the total number of chess books published. Half a century ago, one respected columnist suggested the total number to be 20,000 and if that figure is correct then there must surely be at least 100,000 today. It is a sobering thought that my collection of chess books constitutes perhaps 1% of the total! If these figures are accurate, it is easy to believe the oft-quoted assertion that more books have been published on chess than on any other game or sport. The question as to how many of these books are worth reading is another matter, but the same comment can doubtless be made about any subject.

The introduction of the computer has produced a dramatic change in the way chess information is organized. Hitherto, searching for games involved burrowing into books and magazines, and tracking down one obscure reference could take hours. These days, however, it is all much easier. Databases of games can be obtained from commercial vendors, indexed according to all sorts of criteria. One database I have in front of me, the popular *Mega Database 2010*, contains 4,463,293 games. I decided to look at some other games by Al Modiahki, the winner of the above game. In less than two seconds, the computer informed that he had 924 games in the database. I then wondered if anyone else had suffered the same fate as Tin Htun Zaw, so I set up the position after Black's 5th move in the above game, and then searched the database for all games reaching the same position. This is a harder question, but still the computer only took a few seconds to inform me that the same position had arisen in 20 games (including the above case). Curiously, White found the extremely strong reply 6 ♘f3-g5 in only three of these 20 games, and all three of these games ended in wins for White. However, the computer also informed me that just a few months after the above game was played, it was repeated (up to White's 7th move) in a game played in Vienna. In this later game, however, Black saw the fate awaiting him and resigned straight away.

Computer databases are obviously wonderful tools for the professional player, but they are more generally useful. You can play over the games of the great historical players, conduct research on the various statistical aspects of chess, build up a database of your own games – the possibilities are almost endless. If you are interested in databases, there are specialized chess database programs available (*ChessBase* being one of the most popular) but these days many of the playing programs (such as *Fritz*) have some database functions built in. One word of warning: don't believe everything your computer tells you. Almost all the games in commercial databases were at some stage entered by a human being, and so mistakes are inevitable. So if you play over a game on your computer and see a grandmaster apparently giving his queen away for nothing, and his equally strong opponent not noticing, then it may not really have happened!

Exercises

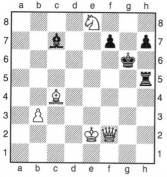

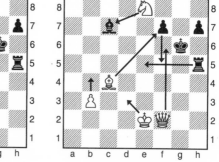

1) List the squares occupied by the various pieces in the diagram above.

2) Write the moves indicated by arrows in chess notation.

3) Play over the following game on a board or computer screen; compare your final position with that given in the solutions: 1 d2-d4 ♘g8-f6 2 c2-c4 g7-g6 3 ♘g1-f3 ♗f8-g7 4 ♘b1-c3 d7-d5 5 c4xd5 ♘f6xd5 6 e2-e4 ♘d5xc3 7 b2xc3 c7-c5 8 ♗c1-e3 ♕d8-a5 9 ♕d1-d2 ♘b8-c6 10 ♖a1-b1 c5xd4 11 c3xd4 0-0 12 d4-d5 ♗g7-c3 0-1

Solutions to Exercises

1) White's pieces: king on e2, queen on f2, bishop on c4, knight on e8, pawn on b3.

Black's pieces: king on g6, rook on h5, bishop on c7, pawns on f7 and h7.

2) Unless you were good at drawing the figurines, you probably wrote Ke2-d3, b3-b4, Ne8xc7, Bc4xf7+, Qf2-f6#, ...f7-f5 and ...Rh5-e5+.

3) The final position is as follows:

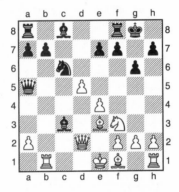

This was a game played between Mikhalchishin (White) and Romanishin (Black) in the 1981 USSR Championship, held in Frunze.

White resigned because Black's bishop is pinning White's queen against his king. Therefore White will lose his queen in return for at most a bishop and a knight. As we shall see, a queen is worth a lot more than a bishop and a knight and, between grandmasters (as these players are), there is no point in carrying on with such a material disadvantage. The move 12 d4-d5?? was an unusually bad blunder for a grandmaster.

4 Winning Your First Games

How are chess games won? We have already stated that the object of the game is to mate the opposing king, so it seems that this question has already been answered. However, mating a well-defended king is far from easy. Of course, if your opponent recklessly exposes his king, then you have good chances of winning without more ado, but you cannot expect many opponents to be so cooperative. Here are two typical patterns for winning a game of chess:

1) You attack the enemy king directly. At some point your threats against his king are so strong that he has no way to stave off mate.

2) You win one of his pieces, possibly on a part of the board far from his king. You then exchange lots of pieces off to reach a simplified endgame position and then, using your extra material, you promote a pawn. With the resulting extra queen, you have no difficulty in mating your opponent (if he has not already resigned).

Of course, there are many other courses that a game of chess can take, and even these two are not necessarily distinct; for example, you may attack as in the first case, and your opponent is then forced to give away a piece to prevent mate. You then proceed as in the second case.

In discussing these matters, the total collection of pieces and pawns in one side's army is referred to as **material**. If one player has more pieces than his opponent (or more valuable pieces), then he has a **material advantage**. In practice, most games are decided by winning material, as in the second case. The skill required to conduct a successful attack on the king is considerable, especially against tenacious defence, and so, to start with, your games are more likely to be decided by a material advantage.

How do you know if you have a material advantage? It may be obvious if both sides have exactly the same pieces, except that you have an extra bishop, but what about more complex situations? Are a bishop and a pawn together worth more than a rook? What about a rook and a bishop against a queen? In order to answer these questions easily, chess-players have devised a handy point-counting system to assess material balances. This runs as follows:

Pawn = 1
Knight = 3
Bishop = 3
Rook = 5
Queen = 9

Of course, you don't need to add up the total for your entire army; you just need to count the differences between your forces and those of your opponent. Using this, we can answer the questions above. A bishop and a pawn are worth less than a rook, and a rook and a bishop are worth less than a queen. These numerical values are useful in a wide range of positions, but you must also take into account the actual situation on the board. A piece that is very badly placed may be worth far less than its numerical value would suggest. There are also certain combinations of pieces that are especially effective; for example, two bishops, because of the way they complement each other, are usually worth slightly more than the six points suggested by the above table. The table may also give misleading results when a significant number of pawns are involved. For example, it suggests that a queen is worth the same as a knight and six pawns. However, in the vast majority of positions, a queen is worth far more than a knight and six pawns. The reason is that the queen can just attack the pawns and take them off one by one; material is of no value if you cannot avoid losing it. If, however, some of the pawns are far advanced then the situation may be reversed. Indeed, the value of a pawn varies considerably according to how far advanced it is. If a pawn cannot be prevented from promoting, then it is worth far more than one point.

One case that occurs fairly often in practice is that of bishop and knight against rook and pawn. The table suggests these are equal in value, but in most positions a bishop and knight are more effective than a rook and a pawn. There is approximate parity only in endgames where there are many open files for the rook. The same comment applies to two knights against a rook and a pawn, while two bishops outweigh a rook and a pawn in virtually every position.

Because the bishop and knight have more or less the same value, we can often talk about them interchangeably, and the term **minor piece** is often used to mean either a bishop or a knight. A **major piece** is a queen or a rook.

If we refer back to page 63, I mentioned that Grandmaster Mikhalchishin resigned because he faced the loss of his queen for a bishop and a knight. We can now see exactly what a disadvantage this would be. A queen is worth nine points, while a bishop and a knight are only worth six. The difference of three points is equivalent to a full minor piece, more than enough for a grandmaster to win on 'automatic pilot'.

How much extra material do you need to win? The answer is not much, but if your material advantage is small, then the level of skill required to convert it into a win may be high. An extra queen or rook should be enough for a beginner to win. An extra minor piece is more tricky, but with correct play should also be enough for a win. Between masters, two pawns is a decisive advantage, and between grandmasters an extra pawn is enough to win more often than not. It follows that even the humble pawn is important in chess; if you have five and your opponent has six, then you may well be in trouble. I must emphasize that when talking about material advantage, I am assuming that the opponent does not have any compensation. If you are a piece up, but your opponent has an attack on your king which forces mate in a few moves, then the extra material is irrelevant.

Let's take a simple example: you have an extra piece for no compensation. The diagram on the following page shows a typical position, symmetrical except that White has an extra bishop.

Winning such a position is actually quite easy. We'll take the white side and let *Fritz*, the fearsomely strong computer program mentioned earlier, take the black side. The basic principle is that White should try to exchange as many pieces (but not pawns) as possible. At the moment (not counting pawns) White has four pieces besides his king, while Black has three. White can be happy with this 4:3 ratio, but if two pieces on each side were exchanged, the figures would be 2:1, i.e. White would have twice as many pieces as Black, an even better situation. Best of all would be 1:0; White's piece could

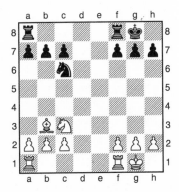

do very much as it liked, since Black would have nothing to oppose it with.

We'll be generous and let *Fritz* have the first move.

1...♖a8-d8 2 ♖a1-d1

White is trying to exchange rooks.

2...♘c6-d4

Fritz attempts to prevent the exchange.

3 ♘c3-d5

This attacks the black knight by cutting off the defence of the rook on d8, and also attacks the pawn on c7.

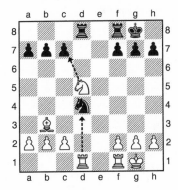

3...♘d4xb3

Fritz acquiesces to the inevitable and exchanges knight for bishop. This is a more or less equal trade.

4 a2xb3 c7-c6 5 ♘d5-e3

The knight has done its duty and retreats. Now rooks are opposed along the d-file and a further exchange of pieces is virtually inevitable.

5...♖f8-e8 6 ♖d1xd8 ♖e8xd8 7 ♖f1-d1

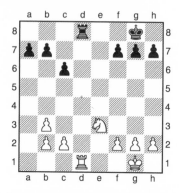

This diagram shows the dilemma faced by a player who is down on material. If Black moves his rook away along the eighth rank, White will jump in with his own rook to d7, where it operates to both left and right, attacking the lined-up black pawns on the seventh rank. Thus Black is faced with a choice of evils: to exchange, or to move his own rook to a passive square while allowing White's to take up an aggressive post.

7...♖d8xd1+

Fritz decides to exchange.

8 ♘e3xd1 ♚g8-f8

White has achieved his target. Now he has only to advance his king and knight, probing for an opening into Black's position. Note that although the king should be kept securely defended when there are many pieces on the board, here Black has nothing that could endanger White's king, so it is perfectly safe to advance it.

9 ♔g1-f1 ♚f8-e7 10 ♔f1-e2 ♚e7-e6 11 ♔e2-e3 h7-h6 12 ♘d1-c3 f7-f5 13 b3-b4 g7-g5 14 f2-f4 g5-g4 15 ♔e3-d4 b7-b6 16 ♘c3-e2 ♚e6-f6 17 ♔d4-c4

White will play his knight to d4, where it attacks the enemy pawns on f5 and c6. Black's king is a short-range piece and cannot defend both pawns at the same time. Thus one black pawn will fall and the end draws nearer.

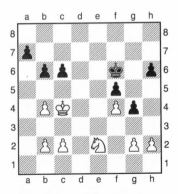

17...a7-a6 18 ♘e2-d4 h6-h5 19 ♘d4xc6 h5-h4 20 ♔c4-d5 b6-b5 21 b2-b3 h4-h3 22 g2-g3 ♔f6-f7 23 c2-c4

Now White will push his c-pawn all the way to the eighth rank.

23...♔f7-f6 24 c4-c5 ♔f6-f7 25 ♘c6-e5+ ♔f7-e7 26 c5-c6 ♔e7-d8 27 ♔d5-d6 a6-a5 28 c6-c7+ ♔d8-c8 29 b4xa5 b5-b4 30 ♘e5-c6 ♔c8-b7 31 ♔d6-d7 ♔b7-a6 32 c7-c8♕+ ♔a6-b5 33 ♕c8-b8+ ♔b5-c5 34 ♕b8-e5#

The important points here are:

1) An extra knight or bishop is usually enough to win. The technique is to exchange as many pieces as possible, win a pawn and eventually create an extra queen. Because pawn promotion is the ultimate aim, you should avoid exchanging too many pawns. In particular, **you should keep at least one pawn**.

2) Patience is often necessary to win games. If you are winning, you don't have to rush, and you don't get any extra points for winning quickly.

3) If you have a winning position and you play well, it doesn't matter how strong your opponent is – he will still lose.

If you have a playing program, try setting up the starting position of this example and see if you can win it yourself. You may find yourself tricked from time to time, but if you are careful then you should find it possible to win.

A great many games end with pawn promotion, or would do if one player did not resign first. Thus the final phase is often a mopping-up operation with the extra queen. In the above example it was quite easy, since White also had an extra knight and could force mate within a few moves. But how do you win with an extra queen if there are no supporting pieces? The technique is actually quite simple.

Here is a typical position.

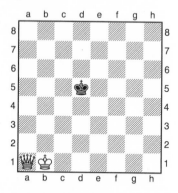

This is even a relatively unfavourable case for White, as his king and queen are tucked away in the corner. The main point is that no mating position is possible with Black's king in the centre of the board, so it is futile to chase the black king round and round aimlessly. In order to mate, White must drive the enemy king to the edge of the board, and the way to do this is not by checking, but by using the king and queen in concert to herd Black's king in the right direction.

1 ♔b1-c2

The win is simplest if White first of all activates his king.

1...♚d5-e6 2 ♔c2-d3 ♚e6-d5 3 ♕a1-f6

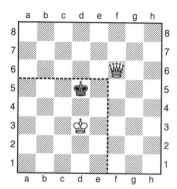

The king and queen are cooperating well. Black's king is confined to a rectangle (dotted lines) and has only one possible move.

3...♚d5-c5 4 ♛f6-e6

Repeating the squeeze. Black's king is approaching the edge of the board.

4...♚c5-b5 5 ♛e6-d6

This shuffling manoeuvre forces Black to the edge of the board.

5...♚b5-a4 6 ♛d6-b6

Now Black's king is trapped in a small box, consisting of the four squares a1-a4. White only needs to bring his king up to finish the job.

6...♚a4-a3 7 ♚d3-c3 ♚a3-a4 8 ♛b6-a6# (or 8 ♛b6-b4#)

The lessons here are:

1) Drive the enemy king to the edge of the board.

2) Confining the king is more important than checking. In the above example, White did not give check at all until the final mate.

3) Be careful not to give stalemate. For example, if White had played 8 ♛b6-c5?? (this really deserves a '??') then Black would have no legal moves, but his king would not be under threat: stalemate.

White has...	Result	Comments
King and knight	Draw	No mating position exists
King and bishop	Draw	No mating position exists
King and two knights	Draw	Mating positions exist, but cannot be forced against competent defence
King and rook	Win	Mate can be forced by driving Black's king into a corner.
King and two bishops	Win	Mate can be forced by driving Black's king into a corner
King, bishop and knight	Win	Mate can be forced by driving Black's king into a corner controlled by the bishop, but skilful play is required

Thus the ending of ♔+♕ vs ♚ is a win, and this is the basic ending of greatest importance, because an extra queen often arises via pawn promotion. White can also win certain other endings without pawns, but the techniques involved are more complicated and we will not cover them in this book. They are rarely required in practice, because you almost always have at least one pawn left which can be promoted. The table on the previous page summarizes the results. In each case, we assume that Black has only his king.

In the next chapter we will discuss how to win material in the first place.

Exercises

1) Which is worth more: a rook or a bishop and a knight?

2) Are two rooks worth more than a queen?

3) White plays the pawn promotion e7-e8♕. How many points of material does this move gain?

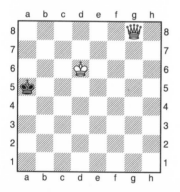

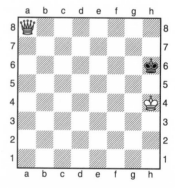

4) White is to play. How can he force mate in two moves?

5) White is to play. How can he force mate in four moves? Here is a hint: you must cut the black king off along the g-file, but at the same time take care so as not to give stalemate.

Solutions to Exercises

1) A rook is worth five points but a bishop and a knight are worth six points, so the rook is less valuable.

2) Two rooks are worth ten points, one more than a queen.

3) The new queen is worth nine points, but at the same time the pawn, worth one point, disappears from the board, so the net gain is only eight points.

4) White can mate in two by **1 ♔d6-c5**. If Black plays 1...♚a5-a6, then White replies 2 ♕g8-a8#, while 1...♚a5-a4 is met by 2 ♕g8-a2#.

5) The correct first move is **1 ♕a8-g2!**, confining the black king along the g-file. Note that 1 ♕a8-g8?? would be a blunder, stalemating Black. The reply **1...♚h6-h7** is forced. Then **2 ♔h4-h5 ♚h7-h8** drives the enemy king into the corner. Now White must again take care, since 3 ♔h5-h6?? and 3 ♕g2-g6?? are both stalemate. **3 ♔h5-g6** is the right choice; after the forced reply **3...♚h8-g8** White plays **4 ♕g2-a8#**. It is curious that White's queen has to return to its original square to deliver the required mate in four.

5 How to Win Material

After having read the last chapter, you might think "That's all very well; if I win a minor piece, then everything is fine. But how do I win material in the first place?" In this chapter we will cover the most common methods of gaining material. You will have to keep the table of piece values given on page 65 firmly in mind, because it is very rarely possible to win something for nothing; your opponent will usually obtain something in return, and you must make sure that you come out ahead.

First of all, let's consider a simple case. You are attacking an enemy piece. Can you take it? If it isn't defended by another enemy piece, then he can't recapture and you can probably take it. Of course, it may be a trap and you should always take care before exploiting what looks like an oversight. However, for the moment we will assume that retribution is not about to strike on some other part of the board and the struggle revolves around whether a particular capture is possible or not.

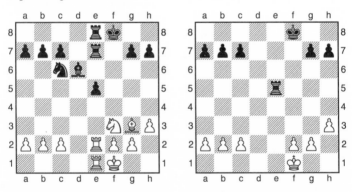

The left-hand diagram is a more complex example. White has several pieces attacking the pawn on e5, and Black has several pieces defending it. Can White take the pawn? The answer is no. Let's imagine that White starts taking on e5. Play might continue **1**

♘f3xe5? ♗d6xe5 2 ♗g3xe5 ♘c6xe5 3 ♖e2xe5? ♖e7xe5 4 ♖e1xe5 ♖e8xe5. The right-hand diagram shows the result: Black is a rook for a pawn up (an advantage of four points). In this sequence, White made matters worse for himself by his capture on move three; up to this point, he had only lost a knight for a pawn (two points) but he then doubled his deficit by giving away further material. We could have guessed that this sequence would turn out badly for White by counting the pieces in the left-hand diagram: White has four pieces attacking e5, and Black has four pieces defending it. In order to take a particular piece, you normally need **more attackers than the opponent has defenders**. If, for example, we move Black's knight one square to the left, then it is no longer defending the pawn on e5. There are now four attackers and only three defenders, so White can safely take the pawn.

However, the advice given above in bold is not the only factor determining the outcome of a sequence of exchanges. The relative value of the attacking and defending pieces is also important, as is the order in which the captures are made.

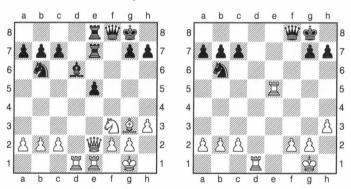

The left-hand diagram is similar to the previous position. White has four pieces attacking e5, and Black has only three pieces defending. One might think that White could take the pawn, but look at what happens if he does: 1 ♘f3xe5 ♗d6xe5 2 ♗g3xe5 ♖e7xe5 3 ♕e2xe5 ♖e8xe5 4 ♖e1xe5. Now we have the right-hand diagram. White has two rooks and a pawn (11 points) in return for a queen and a knight (12 points), so Black has come out ahead. The reason for this is that one of the pieces White used to take on e5 was his queen, which was more valuable than any of the pieces Black surrendered on the same square.

Thus, although the counting advice gives you an indication as to whether a particular capture might succeed, you may have to look at the series of exchanges in more detail to evaluate the result properly. Note that when such a series of exchanges takes place, it is usually best to capture with the **least valuable piece currently available**. Thus as the exchanges proceed, the two players work their way up from the least valuable to the most valuable. The reason for this is that if you take with a more valuable piece first, you opponent may just capture that piece with his least valuable one and stop the series of exchanges at that point.

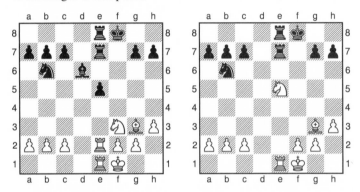

For example, in the left-hand diagram above, White can win a pawn with 1 ♘f3xe5 or 1 ♗g3xe5. However, if White starts with 1 ♖e2xe5?? ♗d6xe5 2 ♘f3xe5 (*see the right-hand diagram*), Black does not continue with the exchanges (which would again leave White a pawn up) but stops here, having gained a rook (5 points) in return for a bishop and a pawn (4 points), leaving him one point up instead of one down.

Readers should note that while there are lots of general principles and helpful tips which apply in a wide range of chess situations, there are **always exceptions**. It is the specific position in front of you that really matters; you should always supplement general considerations with a careful look at the position on the board. This may sound like one of those ubiquitous little legal disclaimers (the author accepts no responsibility for games lost as a result of reading this book...), but there is a valid point behind it. Indeed, it could be said that one of the reasons why some players are so strong is that they can spot precisely those situations in which the normal principles break down, and thereby lead their unsuspecting opponents to their doom.

There are plenty of ways to win material other than by attacking something more times than your opponent can defend it. It is often possible to employ a forcing continuation, often involving checks or captures, to pick up material. The general term **tactics** is used to describe a short-term operation with a concrete aim. A specific operation of this type is usually called a **tactic** or **tactical operation**. The word **combination** has a similar meaning, but is usually used for more elaborate tactical operations, often involving an initial **sacrifice**. The word **strategy** is used for long-term operations with rather less definite aims (for example, a plan to increase the activity of one's bishops would fall under the heading of strategy).

Although tactical operations can be quite complex, they are usually based on a small number of general ideas. The three key ones are:

Double threat: You make two threats at the same time.

Overload: An enemy piece has to do two things at the same time.

Immobilization: A sitting duck is easier to hit than one in the air.

We will see below how a wide range of common tactical devices are based on these basic elements.

Standard Tactical Devices

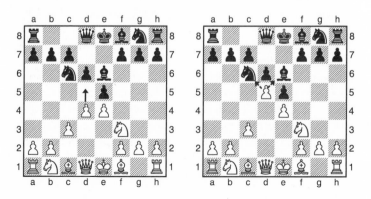

The first of our standard tactical devices is the **fork**. This occurs when one piece simultaneously attacks two or more enemy pieces (and thus falls under the first point above). The left-hand diagram on the previous page is a straightforward example. White advances his pawn, threatening both the c6-knight and the e6-bishop. Black can only move one of the two pieces away, so White is sure to win a minor piece (3 points) in return for a pawn (1 point).

The pawn is not the only piece capable of forking enemy units. **Any** piece has the power to fork, but two are particularly effective: the knight and the queen. The reason is that the actions of both pieces extend in eight different directions, so the chances of catching two enemy pieces on the 'prongs' are enhanced.

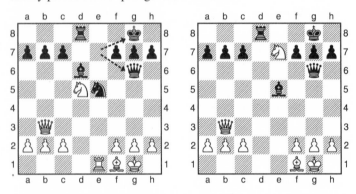

The left-hand diagram shows the knight in action. An experienced player would already observe the makings of a knight fork in the position. The dotted arrows show how a knight landing on e7 would simultaneously check Black's king and attack his queen. If Black had to respond to the check by moving his king, then White would be free to win Black's queen in return for the knight. So why can't White play ♘d5-e7+ immediately? Because Black's bishop is covering this square and 1 ♘d5-e7+? would allow 1...♗d6xe7. True, White would not lose a piece because of 2 ♖e1xe5, but White has a much stronger move than 1 ♘d5-e7+, namely **1 ♖e1xe5!**. If Black does not recapture, then he remains a piece down, but if he plays **1...♗d6xe5**, then White's knight achieves its ambition and by **2 ♘d5-e7+** forks Black's king and queen. The right-hand diagram shows how this works out.

There are several instructive points to note about this position. White wins by an **overload** followed by a **double threat** (a fork in this case), in other words by a combination of two of the basic tactical elements. The overload arises because Black's bishop has two duties: one to defend the knight on e5; the other to cover e7 and so prevent a knight fork on that square. In order to exploit this, White has to find the correct sequence of moves. 1 ♘d5-e7+ followed by 2 ♖e1xe5 didn't have the desired effect, but playing the moves in the reverse order did. If your intended combination doesn't work, **try playing the moves in a different order**. Notice also how White works with the most forcing moves in chess: checks and captures. Black has no opportunity to act for himself; he is forced along a path determined by White. Forcing sequences deserve special attention, both in looking for a winning line for yourself, and in taking care not to fall victim to your opponent's designs.

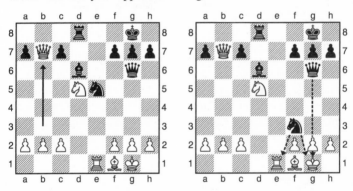

There is one final point to make before we leave this position. Why can White not simply take off the undefended pawn on b7? Of course winning a pawn is not as good as winning a piece, but any material gain is desirable. The left-hand diagram shows the situation now.

However, taking this pawn would be a mistake because Black would then have a knight fork of his own. He would play 1...♘e5-f3+ (*see the right-hand diagram*), both checking and attacking the rook on e1. White could not take the knight with his g2-pawn, because this pawn is pinned by Black's queen. White would have to move his king, and Black would win a rook in return for a pawn. You should always take care to look for your opponent's tactical possibilities as well as your own.

Forks are so common that it is worth looking at another example. This time the queen is the star of the show.

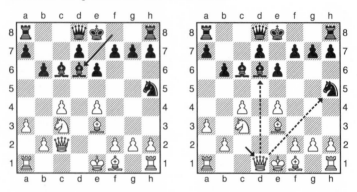

Here is how ex-world champion Anatoly Karpov got caught out by a fork in a game against American grandmaster Larry Christiansen in a tournament played at Wijk aan Zee (Holland) during 1993.

In the left-hand diagram, Karpov (playing Black) has just developed his bishop. However, note that both the d6-bishop and the h5-knight are undefended. Christiansen spotted what Karpov had overlooked: by playing ♕c2-d1 he could fork the two undefended pieces (*see the right-hand diagram*). Black has no way to defend both the attacked pieces, and resigned straight away rather than continue a hopeless struggle a piece down.

A fork doesn't have to be directed against two undefended pieces. One of the 'prongs' of the fork can be aimed against the opposing king. The simplest case is when one 'prong' is actually a check, as in the knight fork on page 79. However, a mate threat, for example, can be equally effective.

In the left-hand diagram on the following page, Black has just played the blunder ...b7-b6??. Why is this wrong? Well, notice the undefended rook on a8. White can't exploit this straight away, but he only has to make a preliminary exchange on f6 to set up the fork. After **1 ♗g5xf6 ♗e7xf6** (it doesn't make any difference if Black plays

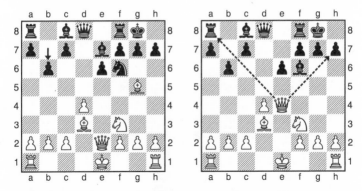

1...g7xf6) White can play **2 ♕e2-e4**. The right-hand diagram shows the situation. White has two threats: 3 ♕e4xh7# and 3 ♕e4xa8. Black must deal with the mate threat, but then he just loses the rook on a8 for nothing.

The position before ...b7-b6?? arises in a common opening variation. Despite this trap being so well known, a search in my database revealed six unlucky victims.

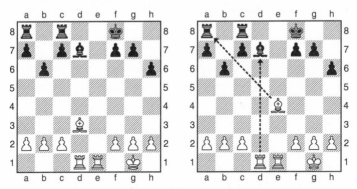

A double attack doesn't have to be a fork. In the left-hand diagram, Black's bishop is undefended and White can exploit this by **1 ♗d3-e4**. This not only attacks the a8-rook directly, it also uncovers an attack along the d-file against Black's undefended bishop. Black cannot avoid losing material (either a piece or a rook for a bishop).

As always in chess, it pays to take care. It appears that White could equally well win material by 1 ♗d3-a6, which also attacks the bishop and a rook. However, in that case Black would even have two ways of escaping from the double attack. He could simply defend the bishop with his rook by 1...♖c8-d8, or he could play the tricky 1...♖c8-e8. In the latter case White could not play 2 ♖d1xd7 because his own rook on e1 would then be undefended, while if he plays 2 ♖e1xe8+ then Black can escape by 2...♔f8xe8 or 2...♗d7xe8.

Many other tactical ideas are special cases of the double attack principle. One of these is the **discovered check**.

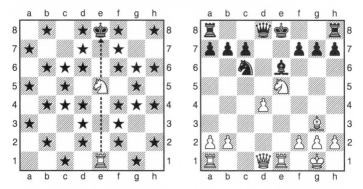

The left-hand diagram shows the skeleton of a discovered check. White has a line-moving piece (in this case the rook) pointing at Black's king, but a friendly piece (here the knight) lies in the way. If this latter piece moves, the black king will be checked by the rear piece. Black will have to attend to the check, so the front piece will have a free move to wreak whatever damage it can – and that can be quite a lot. As we can see from the starred squares in the above diagram, the knight can reach more than half the board in two jumps. If there is any tempting target, for example an enemy queen or rook, on any of these squares, then the knight will be able to capture it.

The right-hand diagram shows how such a discovered check might occur in practice. The line-up of rook, knight and enemy king is just as in the skeleton; the only thing preventing an immediate discovered check is the black bishop on e6. This should lead White to think of a way of removing the obstructing bishop. The key move is **1 d4-d5!**. Since this pawn is attacked twice and only defended once, Black can certainly take it off. However, the penalty is that the bishop is removed from e6, and then the discovered check can strike. The main line is **1...♕d8xd5 2 ♕d1xd5 ♗e6xd5 3 ♘e5xc6+** and White wins a piece with check. Black has no better alternative on his first move: 1...♗e6xd5 2 ♘e5xc6+ costs him his queen, while after 1...♘c6xe5 2 ♖e1xe5 the bishop is pinned against the black king and White can take it with his d5-pawn next move.

A double check is even more compelling than a discovered check, because the opponent has no choice but to move his king. However, the main use of a double check is as part of a mating attack, so we will delay the discussion of this motif until page 124.

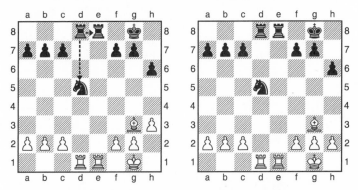

Tactics based on overloaded pieces are also very common. The simplest case is when an enemy piece is defending two other pieces. Then it may be possible to win material by taking the two pieces one after the other. The left-hand diagram above is a case in point. The black rook on d8 has to defend both its colleague on e8 and the knight on d5. By playing **1 ♖e1xe8+ ♖d8xe8 2 ♖d1xd5** White wins a piece. Note that it would be wrong to play these moves in the other order: 1 ♖d1xd5?? would be answered by 1...♖e8xe1+ followed by 2...♖d8xd5, and White would lose two rooks in return for only a knight.

The right-hand diagram is identical, except that White's pawn has been shifted from h3 to h2. Can White still win a piece? The answer is no, because after **1 ♖e1xe8+ ♖d8xe8 2 ♖d1xd5**, Black can play **2...♖e8-e1#** and White would be left ruing his greed. The situation in which the three pawns in front of a castled king are unmoved always demands care, because the pawns prevent the king running away. There is always a danger that at some point an enemy queen or rook will land on the first rank and deliver instant mate (this is normally called a **back-rank mate**). This danger is particularly serious when, as in the above diagrams, there are open files on the board. Sometimes, therefore, players make a small bolt-hole for their king by playing (for example) h2-h3. Whether this is a good idea or not depends on the specific features of the position. The plus-point is the extra security offered; the minus-points are that it consumes a move which might be better spent doing something else, and that it might weaken the king position. Note that the possible weakness of the first rank is much less pronounced after queenside castling, because (assuming White is the one to castle) the king on c1 is not totally blocked in by pawns. Only if White plays ♔c1-b1 does the problem arise, since then the situation is equivalent to that arising after kingside castling.

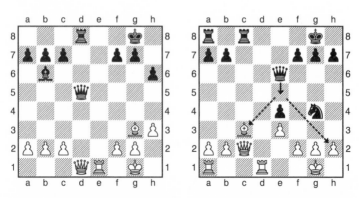

The left-hand diagram features an idea that commonly occurs in practice. Whether you call this an overload or a fork depends on your point of view. It is White to play, and he has the possibility to exchange queens on d5. However, there is a better continuation: **1 ♖e1-e8+!**. You could call this a fork, because the white rook forks the black king and rook, but you could also call it an overload, since the black rook is torn between two duties: to cover Black's first rank and to defend the queen. After 1...♖d8xe8 2 ♕d1xd5 or 1...♔g8-h7 2 ♖e8xd8 White wins material. Although this idea is well-known, grandmasters get caught out by it with surprising regularity. The right-hand diagram occurred in Gelfand-Speelman, from the 1999 FIDE World Championship in Las Vegas. Speelman was to move and he played **1...♕e6-e5**. This was a tricky move, attacking the pawn on h2. If White plays 2 ♗c3xe5, then Black regains the queen by 2...♖c8xc2; he would then even have the advantage, because the e5-bishop and the f2-pawn would both be under attack. However, Black had forgotten about the fork/overload trick. White continued **2 ♖d1-d8+! ♖c8xd8 3 ♗c3xe5 ♘g4xe5 4 ♕c2xe4**, winning a queen and a pawn for a rook and a knight, a gain of two points. This is certainly a decisive advantage between grandmasters and White duly won despite determined resistance by Black.

I have already mentioned pins a few times, but now is the time to do full justice to this useful material-winning idea. If a piece is pinned against the enemy king, then by the laws of chess it cannot move at all (except perhaps along the line of the pin itself).

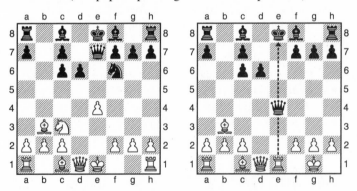

Here is a typical case. In the left-hand diagram, the pawn on e4 is attacked twice by Black's queen and knight, but only defended once. White could defend it again, but instead he plays **1 0-0**. Apparently, this does nothing to prevent Black taking the pawn, but actually it sets a trap. If Black continues **1...♘f6xe4?? 2 ♘c3xe4 ♕e7xe4**, then White continues **3 ♖f1-e1**. The right-hand diagram shows the result. White has pinned Black's queen with his rook. The queen cannot escape, so White has won a queen (nine points) for a rook and a pawn (six points).

It is also possible to pin a piece against something other than the king.

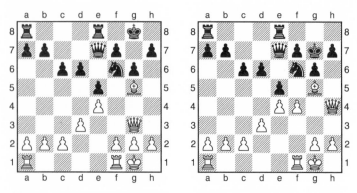

The left-hand diagram shows a knight being pinned by a bishop. White continues **1 ♕g3-h4**. This attacks the pinned knight again. Because a queen is worth far more than a bishop, Black is unable to move his knight. In order to avoid losing the knight, Black must defend it again; the only way to do this is by **1...♔g8-g7**. Now the knight is attacked twice and defended twice; if White were to take on f6, the result would merely be an equal exchange. Therefore, White should step up the pressure against the immobilized knight before Black manages to **unpin** the knight by ...♕e7-e6. The best move is **2 f2-f4**. The right-hand diagram shows the situation now. White's clever pawn move prepares to bring the f1-rook to bear on the pinned knight. The immediate threat is 3 f4xe5, when the multiply-attacked f6-knight must fall. Black has no real answer to this threat and will lose his knight within a couple of moves; after **2...♕e7-e6**, for example, White plays **3 f4-f5**, followed by f5xg6 and again the additional pressure exerted by the rook on f1 proves too much for Black's poor knight. If 3...g6xf5, then 4 ♕h4-h6+ wins.

This example shows how an immobilized piece is a sitting duck. If there is no way of freeing the piece, then it is often doomed. However, a word of caution is necessary. If a piece is pinned against the king, it cannot move by the laws of chess, but if the pin is against another piece, then it can still legally move, and it is worth checking that moves by the pinned piece really do lose material. Suppose, for example, it is Black to move in the left-hand diagram above. Then

Black can reduce much of the pressure against his position by playing **1...♘f6-h5!**. At first sight this looks ridiculous as it just allows **2 ♗g5xe7**. However, Black continues **2...♘h5xg3** regaining the queen, and it becomes apparent that White cannot win any material. This is a case in which the pin can be broken by tactical means, and the impression that the knight cannot move is an illusion.

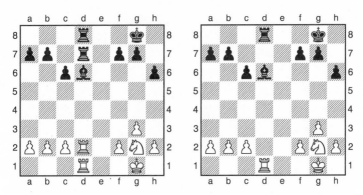

The left-hand diagram above shows another form of pin. In this case the pinning piece is a rook and the piece against which the bishop is pinned is also a rook. Although these two pieces are of equal value, the pin is nevertheless a valid one because Black's d7-rook is insufficiently defended. If the bishop were to move, then the sequence of exchanges on d7 would leave White a rook up. Thus Black cannot move the bishop, nor can he move either rook as then the bishop could be taken for nothing. His only hope to free himself is to play ...♚g8-f8 and ...♚f8-e7 (or ...♚f8-e8), in order to defend the rook on d7 a second time and so free the bishop. However, it is White to move and he has time to bring his knight to bear on the pinned bishop before Black can complete this manoeuvre. White starts with **1 ♘g2-e3!**. This has the double threat (again this important concept) of **2 ♘e3-c4** and **2 ♘e3-f5**. Black can stop the first by ...b7-b5 or the second by ...g7-g6, but he cannot stop both at the same time. Note that after **1...♚g8-f8 2 ♘e3-f5**, the knight controls the e7-square, which the black king would need to defend the bishop again.

In a situation like this, you have to be really sure that the pinned piece cannot move. The right-hand diagram above is superficially similar, but this time White is unable to win material. After **1 ♘g2-e3**, Black plays **1...♗d6-e7**, showing that the 'pin' was not a genuine one.

Our next tactical device, the **skewer**, is a kind of backwards pin.

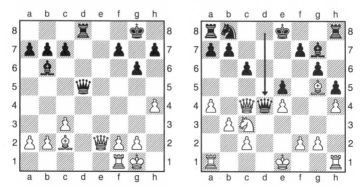

The left-hand diagram shows the basic idea. Black's queen and rook are lined up, a factor which White exploits by **1 ♖f1-d1**. The queen has to move, but is unable to do so in such a way as to defend the rook on d8. Thus White either wins a queen for a rook (4 points), or a whole rook (5 points). In a pin, it is the less valuable piece that is nearer the pinning unit; the situation is reversed in a skewer.

The right-hand diagram shows a real-life situation, from the game Fiala-Mocary, Slovakian Championship, Trenčin 1991. Black has just played ...♛d8-d4?, trying to exchange queens. This was a mistake, because White replied **1 ♖a1-d1!**. Black cannot play 1...♛d4xc4 because of 2 ♖d1-d8#, and so the game continued **1...♛d4-b6 2 ♖d1-d8+ ♛b6xd8 3 ♗g5xd8 ♚e8xd8 4 ♛c4xf7**, when White had a decisive material advantage. In this case, the queen was skewered against the possibility of mate on d8.

Another common way to win material is called **removing the guard**. This motif is really too simple to fit into our scheme of tactical elements, but it is certainly important in practice. The basic idea is straightforward: if one enemy piece defends another, the removal of the supporting piece will leave the other piece vulnerable to capture.

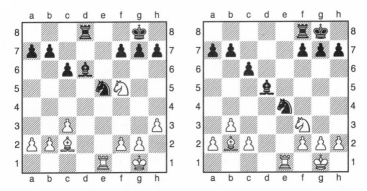

The left-hand diagram shows the idea. White could take Black's knight with his rook, except that it is defended by the black bishop. A preliminary exchange removes the bishop, and then the knight can be freely captured: **1 ♘f5xd6 ♖d8xd6 2 ♖e1xe5**. The right-hand diagram shows a version of this theme. This time the supporting bishop cannot be captured, but it can be driven away by **1 c2-c4**. The bishop is attacked and it has only one safe square to move to, namely e6. This leaves the knight undefended and White can simply take it.

Finally, a piece can simply be trapped, i.e. be attacked and have no safe place to move to. This can easily happen to pieces that unwisely venture into enemy territory without adequate support.

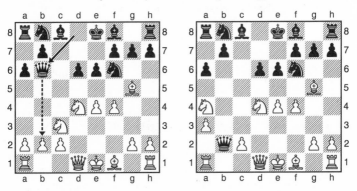

In the left-hand diagram, Black has just played ...♛d8-b6, attacking the undefended pawn on b2. One reasonable reply is **1 a2-a3**, which sets a cunning trap. If Black greedily snatches the pawn with **1...♕b6xb2??**, then the surprising reply **2 ♘c3-a4** traps the queen (*see the right-hand diagram*). The preliminary a2-a3 was necessary as otherwise the queen could have escaped to a3 or b4.

Even a piece in your own half of the board can be trapped if its movement is restricted.

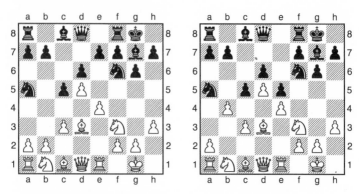

The left-hand diagram occurred in the game Leko-Ehlvest, from a rapid tournament (see page 187) at Cap d'Agde in 1996. Black, to play, has a potential problem with his knight on a5 as it has no moves. Therefore he has to take care that White doesn't trap it by b2-b4. In fact, it is hard to say whether 1 b2-b4 is a threat, because the reply 1...c5xb4 2 c3xb4 ♘f6-d7 would counterattack the rook on a1. Play would then become very complicated. Black, a strong Estonian grandmaster, continued **1...e7-e5??**. This blocks the diagonal from g7 to a1, and so removes any inhibitions White might have felt about advancing his b-pawn. After **2 b2-b4** (*see the right-hand diagram*) Black will lose his knight for a pawn, and so he immediately resigned.

How to Avoid Being Caught Out

We have dealt with all these tactical motifs from the attacker's point of view, but of course it is just as important not to allow your opponent to spring one of them on *you*. Every chess-player, from beginner up to grandmaster, will occasionally overlook a tactical idea, so you should not become frustrated by the occasional unfortunate experience.

However, if such accidents befall you regularly then perhaps you are not taking enough notice of the warning signals, which are often visible before the blow actually falls.

Typical warning signals are:

1) Undefended pieces. If you have two or more undefended pieces, then a fork or double attack may be in the offing. If your king is exposed to checks, then even one undefended piece makes you vulnerable to a fork.

2) Pinned pieces. A pinned piece is usually a serious liability, unless it can be unpinned very quickly. Once the pressure starts to mount against the pinned piece, your other pieces will probably become tied up just defending the pinned piece – which you may lose in the end anyway.

3) Pieces with limited mobility. If a piece has no moves, then it is vulnerable to being trapped. This applies particularly to pieces that can be attacked by an enemy pawn, and to pieces that have ventured into enemy territory.

Here are real-life examples of players coming to a sticky end as a result of ignoring these warning signals.

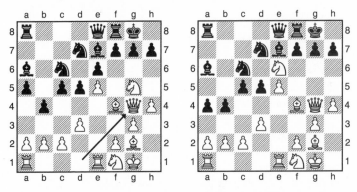

Our first example is from the game Bronstein-Uhlmann, Moscow 1971. White has just played ♕d1-g4 and now Black, assuming that White wasn't threatening anything, continued his queenside advance by **1...a5-a4??**. He had not taken into account the warning signal: undefended knight on c6. White played **2 ♘g5xe6** (*see the right-hand diagram*) and Black faced considerable material loss. White threatens both 3 ♕g4xg7# and 3 ♘e6xf8, so Black has to take the knight, but after 2...f7xe6 3 ♕g4xe6+ White is forking the king and the c6-knight. The result is that Black loses two pawns for nothing, so he resigned immediately. At the time Uhlmann was a leading grandmaster, so his blunder was quite surprising.

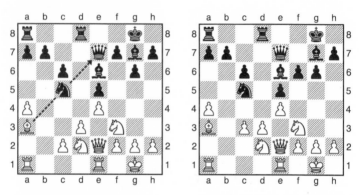

The left-hand diagram arose in the game King-Klundt, Kecskemet 1988. The black knight on c5 is awkwardly pinned, and Black's priority should have been to free it as soon as possible. He could have achieved this by playing ...b7-b6 to defend the knight, followed by moving his queen off the line of the pin. Instead Black played **1...f7-f6??** and after **2 c2-c3** (*see the right-hand diagram*) he resigned. The reason is that White threatens 3 d3-d4 winning the immobilized knight. Black cannot prevent this, since 2...♖d8xd3 loses a piece to 3 ♗a3xc5 (removing the guard).

The left-hand diagram on the following page occurred in I.Novikov-Finegold, New York 1993. Black's queen has gone on a lonely journey into White's half of the board, but it is Black's turn to move and he could have brought the queen back to safety by 1...♕f3-h5. Instead, he ignored the possible danger to the queen and played **1...0-0-0??**. White continued **2 ♗f1-e2** (*see the right-hand diagram*) and Black immediately resigned. The queen has only two squares to avoid immediate capture, but after 2...♕f3-h3 3 ♗e2-g4+ White wins the queen with a fork, while after 2...♕f3-f5 3 ♗e2-g4 the queen perishes to a pin.

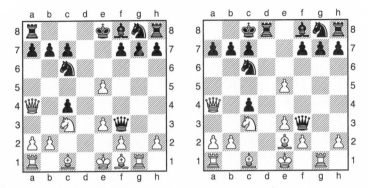

Such is the drastic fate that can await you if you do not pay enough attention to your opponent's threats and ignore the warning signs in your own position.

There are plenty of exercises for this chapter, because the topics covered include some of the most common game-winning ideas. If you do not want to tackle any of the other exercises in the book, at least make sure that you have a go at these. All the following positions are from actual games, and in most cases the losers were players of at least international master strength. The two lessons to be learned from this are:

1) It is very easy to make mistakes in chess. You should always take care, and pay attention to the warning signs mentioned above.

2) Even very strong players sometimes make serious errors. You should not be intimidated when facing a dangerous opponent; he can easily go wrong, just as the players in the examples following did. Your job is to stay alert, so that if he gives you a chance you don't overlook it.

Exercises

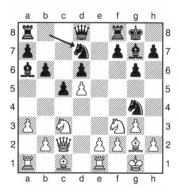

1) This position is from Korotylev-Kiselev, Moscow Championship 1996. Black has just played ...♘b8-d7?. Spot the undefended black pieces and work out how White can exploit them.

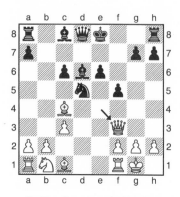

3) In the game Plachetka-J.Přibyl, Czechoslovakian Championship, Frenstat 1982, White has just retreated his queen from e4 to f3. What did Black play next?

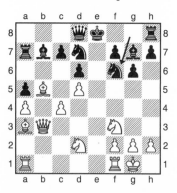

2) Black has just played ...♘g8-f6 in this position from Lputian-Alexandria, Biel 1997. In playing this move she overlooked White's threat. What did White play now?

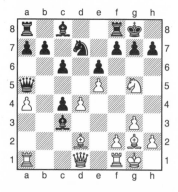

4) In this position from Sorokin-Stavanja, Bled 1992, Black has just snatched a white pawn on c3. How did White exploit Black's greed?

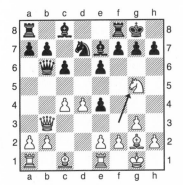

5) This position arose in the game D.Gurevich-Kamsky, Chicago 1989. White has just attacked the e4-pawn, but Black has a strong reply. What is it?

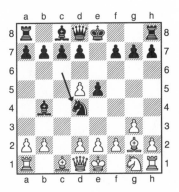

7) In the game Vaulin-Pasztor, Harkany 1994, Black has just played ...♘c6-d4, leaving two pieces exposed. How did White exploit this to win a piece?

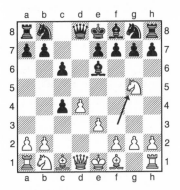

6) Forks can occur at any stage of the game. In this position, from I.Farago-Bliumberg, Budapest 1994, only a few moves have been played, but White unwisely ignored the warning signal 'undefended piece' when he played his last move ♘f3-g5. What did Black play now?

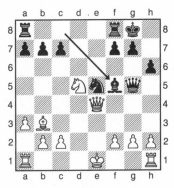

8) In this position from Van Mil-Nijboer, Wijk aan Zee 1992, Black has just played the tricky ...♗c8-f5. If White plays the obvious 1 ♕e4xe5, then 1...♖a8-e8 pins the white queen and wins material. However, White played a different and much stronger move. What was it?

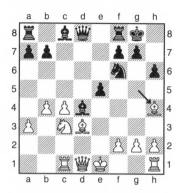

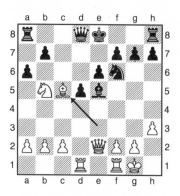

9) This is Rustemov-Lugovoi, Russian Championship, St Petersburg 1998. Here White has just retreated his bishop from g5 to h4. How did Black exploit the fact that it is undefended?

11) This is O.Müller-Vorotnikov, 2nd Bundesliga 1995. White has just played ♗e3-c5, ignoring the attack on his b5-knight. Now 1...a6xb5 can be countered by 2 ♕e2xe5. However, Black found a better move. What was it?

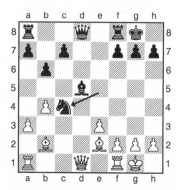

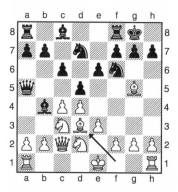

10) In Cherepkov-Anastasian, Leningrad 1990, Black has just played ...♘e5-c4, attacking the bishop on b2. However, this move turned out to be a serious mistake. Why?

12) This is from Kahn-Zifroni, Budapest 1996. White has just played ♗f1-d3. However, he should have been alert to the 'undefended piece' warning. How did Black win material?

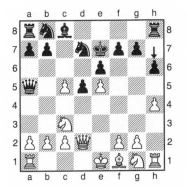

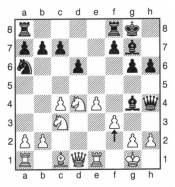

13) This position arose in Velimirović-Ristović, Pozarevac 1995. Black has just played ...h7-h6, overlooking White's main threat. What was it?

15) In Clara-T.Pähtz, Bundesliga 1990/1, White has just met the attack on his queen by playing f2-f3. How did Black now win?

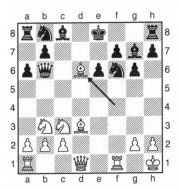

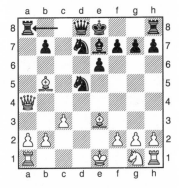

14) This is from Rigo-Martinović, Chianciano 1989. White has just played ♗f4-d6, a combination based on a discovered attack. Black can simply take the bishop by 1...♛b6xd6, but then White was counting on 2 ♗d3-b5+ to win Black's queen. Was this combination correct?

16) In Vorotnikov-Shestoperov, Krasnodar 1991, White has an annoying pin along the a4-e8 diagonal. Black's previous move, ...♖c8-a8, aimed to reduce the effect of this pin by driving away the white queen. However, White exposed a flaw in Black's plan. What did White play?

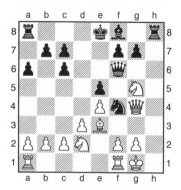

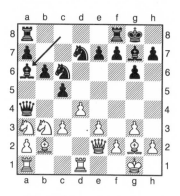

17) White is a piece up in this position from Böhm-Ro.Hernandez, Amsterdam 1979, but it is Black to play. Which white piece is overloaded and how can Black exploit this?

19) In this position, from the game Kasimdzhanov-Cherniaev, Wijk aan Zee 1998, Black made the false assumption that an attacked queen must move. Black has just played ...♗c8-a6. How did White respond?

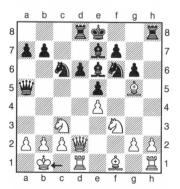

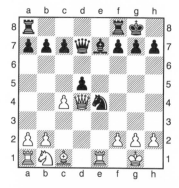

18) This is from Zieher-Kovaliov, Hamburg 1993. White's previous move was ♔c1-b1. This is a normal enough move when castling queenside, but here it was a disastrous error. What did Black play now?

20) Black has just castled in this position from Illescas-Garcia Ilundain, Terrassa 1991. White can take the pawn on d5, but this would merely restore the material balance. Which stronger move did White find?

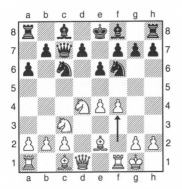

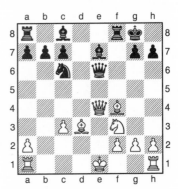

21) In this position from Moskaliuk-Brodsky, Cappelle la Grande 1998, White has just advanced his f-pawn by f2-f4. What was wrong with this move?

23) This is from L.Schneider-Kaiszauri, Stockholm 1980, Black has just castled, relying on the pin of White's queen to prevent ♕e4xh7+. However, Black has missed something. What did White play now?

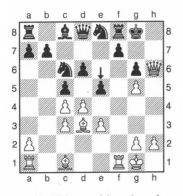

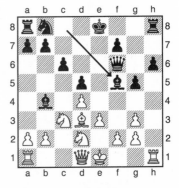

22) This position is taken from Sjöberg-Ornstein, Stockholm 1993. Black's last move was ...e6-e5, but this overlooked White's main threat. How did White now win?

24) In this position from the game Yrjölä-Boguszlavszky, Kecskemet 1987, Black has just played ...♗c8-f5, trying to exchange a pair of bishops. Why was this move a mistake?

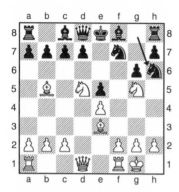

25) Black has just played ...♘g8-h6 in this position from Vogt-Bricard, Wildbad 1990. While White was thinking about his reply, Black suddenly resigned! Evidently Black had spotted the winning move and assumed that his grandmaster opponent would also find it. What should White play?

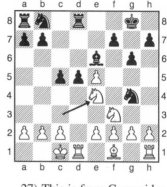

27) This is from Gurgenidze-Azmaiparashvili, Tbilisi 1986. White has just played ♘c3-e4, exploiting his pin of the d5-pawn and aiming for ♘e4xc5, ♘e4-d6 or ♘e4-f6+. Was this move a good idea?

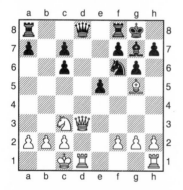

26) This position arose in Kutuzović-Dobrovolsky, Harkany 1994. White is to play. How did he win?

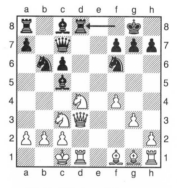

28) In J.Polgar-Rivas Pastor, Dos Hermanas 1993, Black has just played ...♖f8-d8, pinning the d4-knight. How did White win?

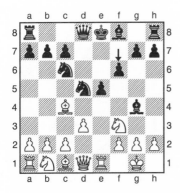

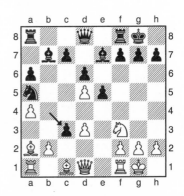

29) This position arose in I.Armas-T.Hartung, Dortmund 1988, after Black's move ...f7-f6. The line-up of the white rook and black king suggests that tactics might be in the air. What did White play next?

31) This position arose in Bezgodov-Vujošević, Balaton-bereny 1996. Black has just captured a white pawn by ...b4xc3, doubtless anticipating the reply b2xc3. However, White played a stronger move. What was it?

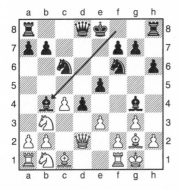

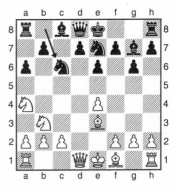

30) This position arose in the game M.Borić-Nikolaevsky, Kiev 1995, Black has just threatened White's queen by playing ...♗f8-b4. What was White's reply?

32) In the game Hector-Vidarsson, Reykjavik 1996, Black has just developed a piece by ...♘b8-c6. What did White play next?

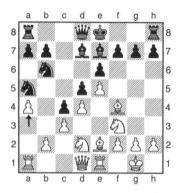

33) White has just played a3-a4 in this position from the game I.Ivanov-Gausel, Gausdal 1993. However, he should have been paying attention to the kingside and not the queenside. What did Black play now?

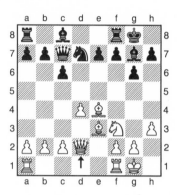

35) Disastrous moves often look so innocent that the player's sense of danger is blunted. In this position, from the game Unzicker-Telljohann, Münster 1993, White has just played the apparently natural move ♕d1-d2. How did Black reply?

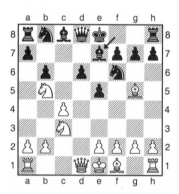

34) Black has just played the developing move ...♗f8-e7 in Adorjan-Zsinka, Budapest 1982. How did White force a quick win?

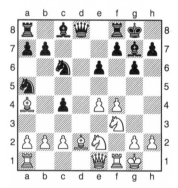

36) It is Black to play in this position from the game Zvara-Mochalov, Pardubice 1996. How did Black use a combination of the two ideas 'trapped piece' and 'fork' to win material?

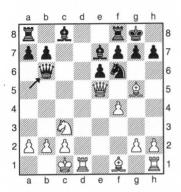

37) This exercise, taken from the game Stisis-Manor, Netanya 1993, is slightly more complicated. Black has just avoided the exchange of queens by playing ...♕a5-b6. How did White win?

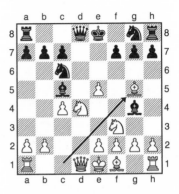

39) In Dietz-Kadas, Kecskemet 1987, White is two pawns up and was probably feeling happy as his last move, ♗c1-g5, attacks Black's queen. How did Black destroy White's good mood?

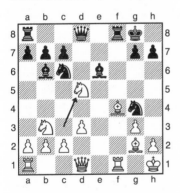

38) This is Lima-Shulman, Erevan Olympiad 1996. White has just played ♘c3xd5 grabbing a pawn. His idea is that the lines 1...♗e6xd5 2 ♕d1xg4 and 1...♘g4-f2+ 2 ♖f1xf2 ♗b6xf2 3 ♘d5xc7 are good for White. How did Black continue?

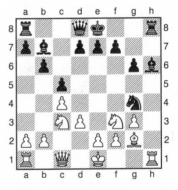

40) This odd position arose in Loginov-Blodshtein, Tashkent 1992. White's queen appears to be under attack from Black's bishop, but in fact Black is not threatening to take the queen as White would reply ♖h1xh8#. How did White continue?

Solutions to Exercises

1) Black's last move left his bishop on a6 undefended. Since the knight on g4 is also without any support, White should be looking for a fork. **1 ♕c2-a4** fits the bill admirably and, on seeing this move, Black resigned.

2) The undefended rook on a7 and the open e-file are clear pointers to White's winning move: **1 ♕b3-e3+** forking king and rook. Black resigned at once.

3) Once again it is an undefended piece which causes all the trouble, in this case the bishop on c4. Black now played **1...♕d8-h4**, threatening ...♕h4xh2# and also attacking the bishop on c4. White resigned as he must lose a piece.

4) White found the decisive fork **1 ♕d1-c2**, threatening both 2 ♕c2xh7# and the bishop on c3. Black must deal with the mate, whereupon he simply loses the bishop for nothing. Black therefore resigned.

5) Here the key weakness is the undefended rook on e1. After **1...♕b6-a5!** this rook is attacked, and since the g5-knight is threatened twice but only defended once, that too is under attack. White realized that he could not escape the loss of a piece and therefore resigned immediately.

6) White obviously wanted to drive away Black's bishop from e6, but he got a shock when Black played **1...♕d8-a5+**, checking the king and attacking the knight on g5. Faced with loss of the knight, White at once resigned.

7) There is no immediate fork, but if White starts with **1 e2-e3**, Black cannot avoid a fork on the following move. If 1...♘d4-b5, then White plays 2 ♕d1-a4, attacking knight and bishop. In the game, therefore, Black moved his knight to the only other available square by **1...♘d4-f5**, but the outcome was similar: **2 ♕d1-g4** forked knight and bishop, winning a piece. Black resigned.

8) White took not the knight but the bishop. After **1 ♕e4xf5** Black resigned, because 1...♕g5xf5 2 ♘d5-e7+ is a knight fork leaving White with a clear extra piece. This was an example of one of the most common errors in chess: focusing on your own tactical possibilities and thereby overlooking your opponent's.

9) Black played **1...♗d4xc3+** and White resigned, because after 2 ♖c1xc3 ♕d8-d4 Black is forking two undefended pieces: the bishop on h4 and the rook on c3.

10) Once again, a preliminary exchange is necessary before the fork actually appears on the board. White played **1 ♗e2xc4** and Black immediately resigned, because he saw that after 1...♗d5xc4 2 ♕d1-g4, White would be both attacking the undefended bishop on c4 and threatening mate by ♕g4xg7#.

11) Black played the clever move **1...♗e5-b8**. Now the knight on b5 is truly attacked, so White must retreat it to avoid losing a piece. It doesn't matter where the knight goes (d4, c3 and a3 are all possible), as in every case Black continues 2...♕d8-c7, both attacking the undefended bishop on c5 and threatening 3...♕c7-h2#. White cannot avoid losing a piece, so he resigned.

12) Black set up a double attack by **1...d5xc4**, attacking both the bishop on d3 and the undefended bishop on g5, and thereby won a piece. Not surprisingly, White resigned straight away. In my database I found seven other examples of exactly the same blunder, so there must be something especially deceptive about the position.

13) For an experienced player, the geometrical line-up of White's queen and Black's undefended queen is a warning signal. White now played the discovered attack **1 ♘c3xd5+** and Black resigned. Black has to deal with the check, and then White simply takes the enemy queen.

14) No, it wasn't a good idea because it contained a major hole. Black did in fact take the bishop by **1...♕b6xd6** and White suddenly realized that his intended 2 ♗d3-b5+ could be met by 2...♔e8-e7!

and White does not win the queen after all. Since White was now a piece down for nothing, he resigned immediately.

15) White's last move opened the diagonal from h4 to e1, with the result that his queen is now overloaded. In addition to defending the knight on d4, it also has the duty of covering the rook on e1. Black now played **1...♗g7xd4+** and White resigned.

16) Black had not taken into account the fact that his queen is overloaded. It has to defend both the knight on d7 and the rook on a8. White exploited this by **1 ♗b5xd7+**. Black resigned as 1...♕d8xd7 allows White to take the rook on a8. At first sight, it looks as though White might not be able to keep the extra piece after 1...♔e8-f8 2 ♕a4-b5, but in fact Black cannot regain the lost material, e.g. 2...♖a8-a5 3 ♕b5xb7 or 2...♘d5-c7 3 ♕b5-d3.

17) White's queen on g4 is overloaded. It must both defend the knight on g5 and cover the square e2 to prevent Black playing ...♘f4-e2#. Black exploited this by playing **1...♕f6xg5**, not only regaining the lost piece but also putting White in serious trouble. If now 2 ♕g4-f3, then 2...♕g5xg2+ 3 ♕f3xg2 ♘f4-e2# again exploits the overloaded queen. The only way White can avoid losing his queen is by 2 f2-f3, but then 2...♘f4-h3+ 3 g2xh3 ♕g5xe3+ 4 ♖f1-f2 (or else White loses the knight on d2) 4...♗f8-c5 sets up a terrible pin along the diagonal from c5 to g1, and this will cost White a lot of material. Therefore White resigned straight away.

18) White had not noticed that his knight on c3 is overloaded. It must defend the pawn on a2, or else Black could force mate by ...♕a5xa2+ followed by ...♕a2-a1#. Therefore it cannot also defend the pawn on e4. Black exploited this by **1...♘f6xe4** and White immediately resigned. The best he can manage is 2 ♕d2-e3 ♘e4xc3+ 3 ♕e3xc3, but after 3...♕a5xa2+ White loses two pawns and his position is shattered.

19) White did not move his queen. Instead he observed that Black's queen is overloaded, since it must defend both the bishop on a6 and the knight on c6. After **1 ♗g2xc6** Black could not avoid loss

of material. 1...♕a4xc6 2 ♕e2xa6 is hopeless, so the only chance is 1...♝a6xe2 2 ♝c6xa4 ♝e2xd1 3 ♖a1xd1, when White has won a bishop and a knight for a rook. Although White is theoretically just one point ahead, in this position, where there are no open lines for Black's rooks, it is undoubtedly a decisive advantage. Black therefore resigned immediately.

20) Before castling, the black queen was defended by the king, but now the queen lacks any support and so the d5-pawn is pinned. White exploited this by **1 ♖e1xe4**, winning a piece for nothing. Black promptly resigned.

21) The advance of the f-pawn opened up the a7-g1 diagonal leading to White's king. This gave Black the opportunity to win by means of a pin. After **1...♘c6xd4 2 ♕d1xd4 ♝f8-c5** White, faced with the loss of his queen, resigned.

22) White played **1 ♝d3xg6** and Black resigned. White threatens mate by ♕h6-h7#, and Black cannot take the bishop because of the pin along the f-file: 1...f7xg6 2 ♖f1xf8# is mate. In fact, Black will be mated in two more moves at the latest, so he resigned.

23) White played **1 ♝d3-c4** and Black resigned. The new pin along the diagonal from c4 to g8 costs Black his queen. This blunder probably had a strong psychological element. Before castling, White was not able to move his bishop along the f1-a6 diagonal because it needed to defend the white queen. When Black castled, the situation changed and suddenly White *was* able to move his bishop. **Every move changes the situation on the board**; what you thought last move may no longer be valid. When a new situation arises, it is often the player reacting most quickly who wins.

24) The undefended queen on f6 means that White can set up a deadly pin by **1 ♕d1-f3**. On seeing this move, Black resigned as he must lose a piece.

25) The crucial factor is the pin of the d7-pawn by White's b5-bishop. This means that it is possible to play 1 ♘g5-e6, attacking

Black's queen. The queen is almost trapped, and the only escape-route is by 1...♕d8-h4. Then White can simply win a rook for nothing by 2 ♘e6xc7+ followed by ♘c7xa8 or, perhaps even better, first play 2 g2-g3, further harassing Black's queen.

26) There is already a pin in the diagram, as the f6-knight cannot move. White's aim must be to step up the pressure against this knight as quickly as possible. He started by **1 ♕d3-f3**, which not only attacks the knight again, but also gains time, as Black must deal with the discovered attack on his queen from the rook on d1. Black resigned here, but had he continued with 1...♕d8-e7 (the only square from which the queen can continue to guard the knight), then 2 ♘c3-e4 would have attacked the knight a third time, to which Black would have had no reasonable reply.

27) No, it wasn't a good idea. When playing a move based on a pin, you have to be careful that your opponent cannot nullify the pin in a way that leaves you in an awkward situation. Here Black played **1...♘b8-d7**, which unpins the d5-pawn and so genuinely threatens to take the e4-knight. The problem is that if the knight moves, then Black can reply ...♘g4xf2, not only winning a pawn but also forking White's rooks. In fact, White is bound to lose at least a rook and a pawn in return for a knight. This is such a large material loss that he decided to resign immediately.

28) It turns out that the pin can be broken in such a powerful way that, far from losing material, White actually wins some! Judit Polgar continued **1 ♘d4-b5!**, with a double attack against Black's queen and the rook on d8. After the forced sequence 1...♖d8xd3 2 ♘b5xc7 ♖d3xd1+ 3 ♘c3xd1 (attacking both the a8-rook and the c5-bishop) 3...♗c5xg1 4 ♘c7xa8 White will end up with a rook and a pawn for a bishop. Since this material advantage is enough for an easy win, Black decided to shorten his agony and resigned at once.

29) White found a decisive combination based on a discovered check. He played **1 ♘f3xe5!**, the main point being that after 1...♗g4xd1 White regains the queen by 2 ♘e5xc6+ ♗f8-e7 3 ♘c6xd8 ♖a8xd8 4 ♖e1xd1 and makes off with an extra piece. In fact, Black

has nothing better than 1...♘c6xe5 2 ♕d1xg4, but then he is a pawn down, his knight is awkwardly pinned and his king is still stuck in the centre. White should certainly win from this position, so Black decided to cut proceedings short and resign straight away.

30) The b4-bishop is defended only by the knight on c6, a piece which White can eliminate with his g2-bishop. White played **1 ♗g2xc6+** and Black, faced with the loss of a piece, resigned. Here it is important that the capture on c6 is check, for otherwise Black could simply ignore the capture and take White's queen instead.

31) Instead of recapturing, White played **1 b2-b4** trapping the knight on a5. Faced with the loss of a piece, Black resigned.

32) Black must have had a total blackout to have missed White's main threat. After **1 ♗e3-b6** Black resigned, as his queen is lost.

33) Black played **1...g7-g5** and White resigned. It doesn't matter whether the bishop retreats to e3 or g3; in either case, Black continues 2...g5-g4 and traps the knight on f3. Since White is losing a piece no matter what he plays, he decided to resign.

34) The key here is the exposed black rook on a8. If White could attack it along the open h1-a8 diagonal, then it would be trapped. White achieved this by **1 ♗g5xf6 g7xf6** (taking back with the bishop is no better) **2 ♕d1-d5**. Black tried to keep his losses down to a piece by playing **2...♘b8-c6 3 ♕d5xc6+ ♗c8-d7**, but at this point he resigned before White had a chance to play 4 ♘b5-c7+ followed by 5 ♕c6xa8 (or 4 ♕c6xa8 first).

35) Perhaps surprisingly, White's queen move cost him a piece after **1...f7-f5**. The bishop on e4 has only one escape square, but after 2 ♗e4-d3 f5-f4, the other bishop has none! White therefore resigned. This just shows that there is no completely safe position in chess, and even if there doesn't appear to be any danger, you still have to keep an eye open for your opponent's possibilities. The player who had White in this game is an experienced grandmaster, but he let his guard down for a moment, with fatal consequences.

36) Black found a quick one-two to knock White out. The first blow was **1...b7-b5** attacking the a4-bishop, which is very short of squares. White resigned here, because after 2 ♗a4xb5, the second punch lands: 2...♕d8-b6+, forking king and bishop. If White plays 2 ♗d2xa5 instead, then Black continues 2...♘c6xa5 and the situation remains essentially the same: White must lose a piece.

37) White played **1 ♘c3-a4**, attacking the enemy queen. The queen appears to have many squares open to it, but in fact it is trapped and can only escape at the cost of a piece. If Black plays 1...♕b6-b4, then 2 ♖d1-d4 rounds up the queen, while 1...♕b6-f2 2 ♖d1-d2 is similar. Therefore, Black chose the only remaining available square: **1...♕b6-c6**. However, **2 ♗f1-b5** proved decisive. After 2...♕c6xg2 (2...♘f6-d7 3 ♕e5-e2 is no better) 3 ♖h1-g1 ♕g2xh2 4 ♗g5xf6 ♗e7xf6 5 ♕e5xf6 Black has avoided losing his queen, but has lost a piece for two pawns instead. In addition, his king is extremely vulnerable and after, for example, 5...g7-g6 6 ♖g1-h1 ♕h2-g2 7 ♖h1-h6 followed by ♖d1-h1 White has a decisive attack. Black therefore resigned. This is another of those deceptively natural blunders – on my database I found five examples.

38) Black played the surprising **1...♕d8xd5!**. Far from winning a pawn, White now loses at least a piece; for example, 2 ♕d1xg4 ♕d5xg2+ 3 ♔h1xg2 ♗e6xg4 or 2 ♗g2xd5 ♗e6xd5+ 3 ♖f1-f3 ♘g4-f2+ 4 ♔h1-g2 ♘f2xd1. White therefore resigned.

39) Black continued with the unexpected **1...♕d8xg5!**. White must lose a piece; e.g., 2 ♘f3xg5 ♗c5-b4+ 3 ♕d1-d2 ♗b4xd2+ 4 ♔e1xd2 ♘c6xd4. In the game White preferred **2 ♘d4xc6**, but resigned after **2...♗g4xf3 3 g2xf3 b7xc6** as he is a piece for two pawns down with, in addition, a very bad position.

40) White decided the game with the surprising move **1 ♕c1-g5!**. Black is still unable to take the queen, and the g4-knight is attacked. This knight cannot move because it must defend the h6-bishop, so Black must defend the knight. The only available method is 1...f7-f5, but allowing White to take the g6-pawn with check is disastrous; for example, 2 ♕g5xg6+ ♔e8-f8 3 ♘f3-g5. Therefore Black resigned.

6 The Enemy King

The enemy king is of prime importance in chess, because its capture is the ultimate object of the game. Indeed, it is a potential target throughout the game. We have already seen in the previous chapter how many tactical ideas become especially effective when the enemy king is involved. For example, pinning a piece against the king guarantees that it cannot move, whereas a pin against another piece might be a 'false' pin rather than a genuine one. A fork involving the king is especially effective, because the opponent *has* to respond to the check. It is the element of compulsion that makes a check such a powerful weapon. However, there is no point in giving aimless checks. Beginners often like to give check; their motto is 'always give a check; it might be mate'. Of course, if it is mate then that is the end of the game, but one should think about whether or not a check is mate before playing the move, not after! Checks are indeed useful if they serve a concrete purpose, for example as part of a tactical operation, in order to drive the enemy king to an inferior square, or to transfer one of your own pieces to a better square with gain of time. **Never check just for the sake of it**.

Attack on the King

I have described on page 64 how games are often won either by the accumulation of material, or by a direct attack on the enemy king. There is no disguising the fact that attacking your opponent's king is more fun. 150 years ago, chess was played as if attacking were all there is to the game. These days, we have a more pragmatic approach. There are indeed some players who don't mind losing nine games if they can win one by a brilliant attack, but such players are very much in the minority (and they don't become grandmasters!). Most players want to score as many points as possible, move up the ranking list, and so on, and always playing for the attack is not the way to achieve this. Having said that, attacking *is* an important part of the game, but you have to be able to recognize when the attack is likely to succeed.

Risks and Rewards

Just as in real warfare, if there are no special conditions present then the odds somewhat favour the defender. There are several reasons for this. First of all, the attacker has to move the pieces involved into the vicinity of the enemy king. This can take some time, which gives the defender a chance to disrupt the operation or even to start a counter-attack. Secondly, sensible players keep their king well defended behind a wall of pawns. This wall has to be breached in order to allow the attacker to engage the enemy king in hand-to-hand combat. Even when the pawn defences have been disposed of, the defender's other pieces may still frustrate the attack. It is also worth bearing in mind that an attack is not exactly a covert operation; normally, you can't disguise the fact that you are feeding your pieces towards your opponent's king. With many chess operations, your opponent may overlook your intentions until it is too late, but this is unlikely with a direct attack.

The launching of an attack is a very committal decision. It is often necessary to invest both time and material in an attack, so once you have started you should not have second thoughts. Even if you have some doubts, remember that even attacks which are not completely correct often succeed in practice. An attack puts pressure on the defender, who often has to come up with a string of good moves to fend off the attack. If these are not forthcoming, then the attack can crash through.

There are several factors that can tip the balance in the attacker's favour, and make the launching of an attack a favourable bet.

1) If your opponent has not castled and his king is in the centre. The reason this improves the odds for an attack is that it is desirable to control the centre of the board in any case (see the section on opening play, page 135). Thus the moves you need to build up your attack also improve your position even if the attack comes to nothing. This greatly reduces the risk factor and often tips the odds in favour of the attacker. It is worth noting that here we are talking about the situation in which the opposing king will have to stay in the centre for a number of moves. If he can castle in one move, then he can wait until the last moment and then suddenly whisk his king away from the danger. At the other end of the spectrum, if the defender has been forced to move his king (without castling) then his castling rights have been permanently forfeited and the attacker will usually be able to prepare his onslaught more slowly, secure in the knowledge that the opposing king will be a long-term target.

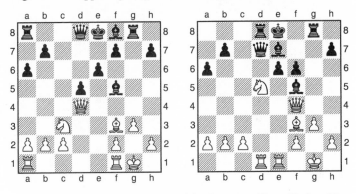

The left-hand diagram occurred in the game Nunn-Tarjan, Norwich Junior 1972. Black certainly cannot castle kingside as he has moved his rook from h8, while it still takes two moves to castle queenside. White's task is to keep Black off-balance and prevent him from safeguarding his king on the queenside. Thanks to the open central files, White can accomplish this while playing natural developing moves which strengthen his position in any case. The game continued **1 ♖f1-e1** (pinning the e6-pawn and so threatening to take the pawn on d5) **1...♗f8-e7 2 ♕d4-e5** (now White threatens to win a pawn by 3 ♘c3xd5 e6xd5 4 ♕e5xf5) **2...f7-f6** (this makes life easy for White, but even after the more solid 2...♗f5-g6 3 ♖a1-d1 ♔e8-f8, the sacrifice 4 ♘c3xd5 e6xd5 5 ♖d1xd5 is still very promising for White) **3 ♕e5-f4** (renewing the threat to take on d5) **3...♕d8-d7** (at last Black threatens to castle...) **4 ♖a1-d1** (...but White can prevent it with another natural developing move which brings his last piece into play) **4...♖a8-d8** (4...0-0-0 also loses to 5 ♘c3xd5 e6xd5 6 ♖d1xd5, forking d7 and f5) **5 ♘c3xd5!** (*see the right-hand diagram*) **5...e6xd5 6 ♖d1xd5 ♕d7-c8** (the point of White's combination is that after 6...♕d7xd5 7 ♗f3xd5 ♖d8xd5, White can play 8 ♕f4-c4 skewering the two black rooks) **7 ♖d5xf5 1-0**. Black resigned at this point because he is two pawns down, while White's attack continues unabated.

The important point about this example is that thanks to the position of Black's king, White was able to generate all his threats with normal developing moves. In the end he was able to sacrifice and break down Black's defensive wall, but even if this had not been possible, the moves he had played would not have been wasted.

2) If there is a major weakness in the pawn-structure in front of the enemy king. This is equivalent to leaving the drawbridge down and inviting the enemy troops in to dinner.

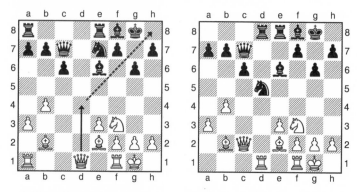

Take a look at the left-hand diagram above. White's kingside pawn-structure is intact. The pawns are next to each other, controlling all the squares along the third rank. This prevents any enemy pieces settling near to the king. In addition, White has two defensive pieces, the f3-knight and the e2-bishop, helping to secure the king. This is a good, solid kingside position without weaknesses.

Black, on the other hand, has a problem. His kingside is weak because his pawn is on g6 rather than g7. This has two negative effects. Firstly, some squares on the third rank are not covered by a pawn. If, for example, White's knight were on e4 rather than f3, White would be able to jump in by ♘e4-f6+, with devastating consequences. Secondly, Black is weak along the a1-h8 diagonal. This is particularly significant here because White's bishop is already in a good position to exploit this weakness. If White is to play in the diagram, then **1 ♕d1-d4** creates the very awkward threat of ♕d4-h8#. Black is hardly able to prevent this, and in order to avoid mate he would have to play something like **1...f7-f6 2 ♕d4xf6 ♘e7-f5**, but after **3 ♕f6-h8+ ♔g8-f7 4 ♕h8xh7+** Black's position has collapsed. Black's weakness along the long diagonal was particularly severe because his minor pieces were very poorly placed to cover the weakened dark squares f6, g7 and h8. His dark-squared bishop would have been best for the job, but it was cowering on f8, while his knight was situated on a dark square, and so was only defending light squares.

If it is Black to move in the diagram, then he can prevent White's queen arriving on the weakened diagonal. A plausible continuation is **1...♖a8-d8 2 ♕d1-c2 ♘e7-d5 3 ♖a1-d1** (*see the right-hand diagram*), when Black has avoided an immediate disaster. However, White retains a small advantage because Black's kingside will always suffer from a slight weakness.

3) If the opponent's king position is devoid of defensive pieces. In this case the pawn barrier may not be enough to hold the attackers off.

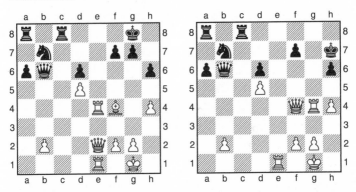

The left-hand diagram arose in Nunn-Greenfeld, London 1984, with White to play. All Black's pieces are far away from his king, which is looking very lonely. On the other hand, all White's pieces are within striking distance of the kingside, with the bishop and rook on e4 in particularly dangerous positions. The game continued **1 ♗f4xh6!** (a sacrifice to break open the black king's pawn-cover) **1...g7xh6 2 ♖e4-g4+ ♔g8-h8** (2...♔g8-h7 3 ♕e2-e4+ ♔h7-h8 4 ♕e4-f4 wins the same way) **3 ♕e2-d2 1-0**. Black resigned as White can force mate by 3...♔h8-h7 4 ♕d2-f4 (*see the right-hand diagram*) 4...♕b6xb2 (or 4...♖c8-c7 5 ♕f4-f5+ ♔h7-h8 6 ♕f5-f6+ ♔h8-h7 7

♕f6-g7#) 5 ♕f4xf7+ ♚h7-h8 6 ♖g4-g6 and Black cannot meet the threat of ♖g6xh6#.

Attacking requires considerable imagination and creativity, but it certainly helps if you are aware of standard attacking ideas and mating patterns. If you win a pawn, the game is far from over, but if a typical mating pattern appears on the board, you can often look forward to a quick finish.

First of all, let's consider the case in which the opposing king is in the centre. In the initial position, Black's weakest spot is the square f7, because it is only defended by the king. Many beginners try to take advantage of this by a crude attack such as 1 e2-e4 e7-e5 2 ♗f1-c4 ♘b8-c6 3 ♕d1-h5.

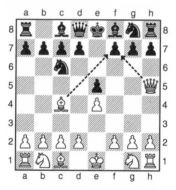

This does threaten mate in one by 4 ♕h5xf7#, but you can't really expect that your opponent will overlook the threat. It is easy to stop the threatened mate, and then White's early queen excursion will turn out to be misguided. For example, after 3...♕d8-e7, followed by ....♘g8-f6, White will have to move his queen again, losing time. 3...g7-g6 is perhaps even simpler; if White renews the threat by 4 ♕h5-f3, then 4...♘g8-f6 stops the mate with a normal developing move, and then ...♗f8-g7 followed by ...0-0 allows Black to complete his kingside development very quickly. You cannot expect to succeed with an attack that is not properly prepared.

However, if your opponent makes a mistake early on, then the circumstances for an attack against f7 (or f2 if Black is attacking White) may arise. Most players are careful to get their king castled early on, but there are always a few who delay this safety measure and get caught out. We have already seen one example in the game M.Al Modiahki-Tin Htun Zaw on page 56 (we will look at this game again on page 163). Here are two more.

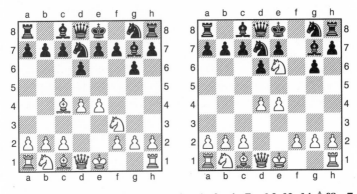

The left-hand position arises after **1 e2-e4 g7-g6 2 d2-d4 ♝f8-g7 3 ♘g1-f3 d7-d6 4 ♝f1-c4 ♘b8-d7??**. White can win by 5 ♝c4xf7+! ♚e8xf7 6 ♘f3-g5+ ♚f7-e8 (6...♚f7-f6 7 ♕d1-f3# is a nice mate) 7 ♘g5-e6 and Black's queen is trapped (*see the right-hand diagram*). A database search in *Mega Database 2010* revealed 73 games which reached the left-hand diagram position, but oddly enough White found the winning combination in only 23 of these, the first occasion being in 1946. In the 23 games in which White took on f7, I was surprised to find Ibragimov-Zhelnin, Moscow 1998, in which a highly-ranked Russian player fell victim to this relatively well-known trap.

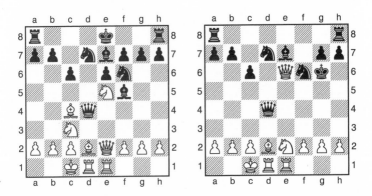

The left-hand diagram on the previous page is a more complicated example, from the game Mitkov-Bacrot, Nice 1994. Black has delayed castling, instead preferring to grab White's d4-pawn with his queen. This turned out to be a serious error as White now struck on the sensitive square f7: **1 ♘e5xf7! ♔e8xf7** (Black could have limited the damage by 1...0-0, but after 2 ♘f7-g5 ♘d7-c5 3 ♗c4xe6+ ♘c5xe6 4 ♘g5xe6 ♗f5xe6 5 ♕e2xe6+ Black would be a pawn down with a bad position) **2 ♗c4xe6+ ♗f5xe6** (2...♔f7-g6 3 ♗e6xf5+ ♔g6xf5 4 ♕e2-f3+ ♔f5-g6 5 ♖e1xe7 is hopeless, as White is a pawn up with a tremendous attack) **3 ♕e2xe6+ ♔f7-g6 4 ♘c3-e2** (far stronger than immediately regaining the piece on e7; White swings his knight into the attack) **1-0** (*see right-hand diagram*). Black resigned as after 4...♕d4-g4 5 ♘e2-f4+ ♔g6-h6 6 ♕e6xe7 White is already material ahead, and his coming discovered check will gain further booty.

The possibilities for attacking the king after castling are rather more varied, and we will look first at the concluding phase of the attack, when mate is already close. There are certain standard mating patterns that occur time and time again in practice; familiarity with these is a big point-winner. In each case we show a skeleton of the mating idea and a practical example.

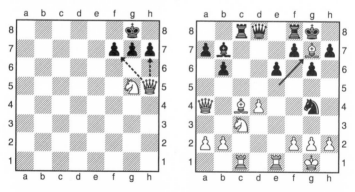

We can see the basic idea in the left-hand diagram. White's queen and knight cooperate in a simultaneous attack on f7 and h7. It is important that the threat to f7 is a genuine one (i.e. f7 is not defended) or else Black can meet the attack by ...h6. There are several versions of this basic ♕h5 + ♘g5 attack; for example, if Black's h-pawn is missing then the attack on h7 may be hard to meet even if f7 is defended.

The right-hand diagram shows how this attack works in practice. This position is from the game P.Zimmermann-Schmall, Germany 1992/3. White has just played ♗e5xg7, taking off a black bishop. Doubtless he expected the reply ...♔g8xg7, but Black spotted the weakness of f2 and h2 and continued **1...♕d8-h4!**. This threatens mate in two by 2...♕h4xf2+ 3 ♔g1-h1 ♕f2xg2#, and there is a second threat to h2. White has no defence and he was reduced to **2 ♗c4-d5 ♗b7xd5** (2...♖c8xc3 3 ♗d5xb7 ♕h4xf2+ 4 ♔g1-h1 ♖c3xc1 5 ♖e1xc1 ♕f2-f4, threatening both 6...♕h4xh2# and 6...♕f4xc1+, is just as effective) **3 ♘c3xd5 ♖c8xc1 4 ♖e1xc1 ♔g8xg7** (the same theme again; f2 and h2 are still under fire, and in addition the knight on d5 is attacked) **5 h2-h3 ♕h4xf2+ 6 ♔g1-h1**. Black now played **6...♕f2xb2** and won easily enough, but 6...♖f8-c8! would have been even more crushing (as 7 ♖c1xc8 allows 7...♕f2-f1#).

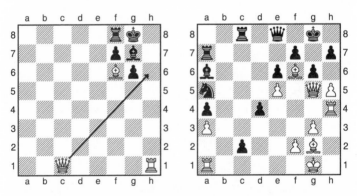

The left-hand diagram shows one typical form of the bishop and rook attack, in which the bishop supports a rook mating on the back rank. White can force mate by **1 ♕c1-h6!**. There are multiple threats; for example, 2 ♕h6xg7#, 2 ♕h6-h7# and 2 ♕h6-h8+ ♗g7xh8 3 ♖h1xh8#. After **1...♗g7xh6 2 ♖h1xh6**, Black is in no position to prevent the bishop and rook mate with ♖h6-h8#.

The right-hand diagram features a slightly different situation in which the black bishop is missing. It arose in Fischer-Mjagmasuren,

Interzonal tournament, Sousse 1967; the great American champion continued 1 ♕g5-h6 ♕e8-f8 2 ♕h6xh7+! and Black resigned since after 2...♔g8xh7 3 h5xg6++ Black is mated either by 3...♔h7-g8 4 ♖h4-h8# (our familiar pattern) or 3...♔h7xg6 4 ♗g2-e4#.

An attack is often greatly strengthened by having a friendly pawn in the vicinity of the enemy king.

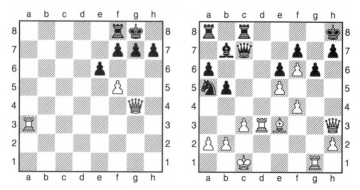

The left-hand diagram is typical. White starts with **1 f5-f6 g7-g6** (forced to avoid immediate mate) **2 ♕g4-g5**. This threatens 3 ♕g5-h6 followed by 4 ♕h6-g7# and Black's only defence is **2...♔g8-h8 3 ♕g5-h6 ♖f8-g8** in order to cover the square g7. If White has a rook ready to move to the h-file (as is the case here) then the most forceful finish is **4 ♕h6xh7+ ♔h8xh7 5 ♖a3-h3#**. In this specific position, 4 ♖a3-h3 also works, but it is generally better to mate with checks if at all possible, since it gives your opponent less chance to interfere with your attack.

The right-hand diagram arose in Pirisi-Van Wely, Sas van Gent 1988. All the elements are in place, except that White's rook on d3 lacks immediate access to the h-file. However, White solved that problem by **1 ♕h3-h6 ♖c8-g8 2 ♗e3-b6!**, getting rid of the bishop with gain of time by attacking Black's queen. Black has no answer to the attack along the h-file and the finish was **2...♕c7xb6 3 ♕h6xh7+ ♔h8xh7 4 ♖d3-h3#**.

A white pawn on g6 can be just as dangerous for Black's castled position.

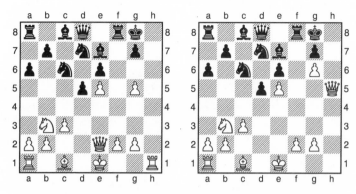

In the left-hand diagram, White has already sacrificed two pieces to remove some of the pawns defending Black's king. White's aim is to establish a formation with queen on h5 and pawn on g6, threatening mate on h7. However, the obvious tries are too slow; for example, 1 g5-g6 ♖f8-f5! prevents ♕e2-h5, while 1 ♕e2-h5 ♘d7xe5 2 g5-g6 ♘e5xg6 breaks up White's mating formation. The correct solution is to sacrifice a rook to set up the required formation with gain of time: **1 ♖h1-h8+! ♔g8xh8** (or 1...♔g8-f7 2 ♕e2-h5+ g7-g6 3 ♕h5-h7+ ♔f7-e8 4 ♕h7xg6#) **2 ♕e2-h5+ ♔h8-g8 3 g5-g6** (*see the right-hand diagram*; Black can only stave off mate for a few moves) **3...♘d7-f6 4 e5xf6 ♖f8xf6 5 ♕h5-h7+ ♔g8-f8 6 ♕h7-h8#**.

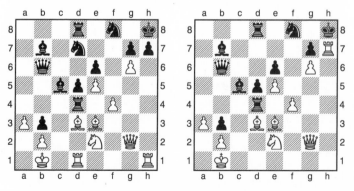

The left-hand diagram, from the game Nunn-Gschnitzer, Bundesliga 1990/1, is another example. Here the attacking pawn is already on g6, but there is still a black pawn on h7, defended by a knight. White has to use drastic measures to break down Black's resistance at h7, but the end result, just as before, is the formation with a pawn on g6 and the white queen on the h-file: **1 ♖h1xh7+! ♘f8xh7 2 ♖d1-h1 ♘d7-f8** (if Black ignores the attack on h7 with 2...♖d4xd3, then White wins by 3 ♖h1xh7+ ♔h8-g8 4 ♖h7-h8+! ♔g8xh8 5 ♕g2-h3+ ♔h8-g8 6 ♕h3-h7+ ♔g8-f7 7 ♕h7-h8+ ♔f8-e7 8 ♕h8xg7+ ♔e7-e8 9 ♕g7-f7#) **3 ♖h1xh7+** (*see right-hand diagram*) **3...♔h8-g8** (or 3...♘f8xh7 4 ♕g2-h3 ♔h8-g8 5 ♕h3xh7+ ♔g8-f8 6 ♕h7-h8+ ♔f8-e7 7 ♕h8xg7+ ♔e7-e8 8 ♕g7-f7#) **4 ♕g2-h3 ♘f8xg6** (the sole way to avoid immediate mate, but it only delays the end by a few moves) **5 ♗d3xg6 ♖d4-d1+ 6 ♘e2-c1 1-0**. After 6...♔g8-f8 7 ♕h3-h4 Black cannot avoid mate.

One mate which occurs quite often in practice is the so-called **smothered mate**, in which one king is totally hemmed in by his own pieces, and the opponent delivers mate with a knight.

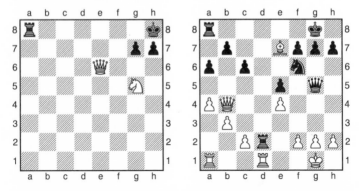

The left-hand diagram shows the basic idea. Black's king is not quite 'smothered' as the square g8 is free. However, White can block the last square by sacrificing his queen: **1 ♘g5-f7+ ♔h8-g8 2 ♘f7-h6++ ♔g8-h8** (or 2...♔g8-f8 3 ♕e6-f7#) **3 ♕e6-g8+ ♖a8xg8 4 ♘h6-f7#**.

Smothered mates can occur in other situations, but this particular pattern occurs surprisingly often in practice. The right-hand diagram features one example, from the game Van Haastert-Miezis, Dieren 1997. Black continued **1...♖d2xf2! 2 ♔g1xf2** (White can avoid mate by 2 g2-g3, but after 2...♖f2xc2 he has lost two pawns) **2...♘f6-g4+** and now White cannot avoid his fate; for example, 3 ♔f2-g1 ♕g5-e3+ 4 ♔g1-h1 ♘g4-f2+ (the familiar pattern appears again) 5 ♔h1-g1 ♘f2-h3++ 6 ♔g1-h1 ♕e3-g1+ 7 ♖d1xg1 ♘h3-f2# or 3 ♔f2-g3 ♕g5-f4+ 4 ♔g3-h4 ♘g4-f6+ 5 ♔h4-h3 ♕f4-g4#. In the game White played **3 ♔f2-f1** and Black went straight for the smothered mate by **3...♕g5-f4+ 4 ♔f1-g1 ♕f4-e3+ 5 ♔g1-h1 ♘g4-f2+ 6 ♔h1-g1 ♘f2-h3++ 7 ♔g1-h1 ♕e3-g1+ 8 ♖d1xg1 ♘h3-f2#**. In fact, Black could have mated more rapidly by 3...♕g5-e3, but you don't get extra points for winning quickly and Black preferred to head for the familiar pattern.

We have already mentioned back-rank mates briefly on page 84. This is one of the most common mating patterns, so here are two typical examples.

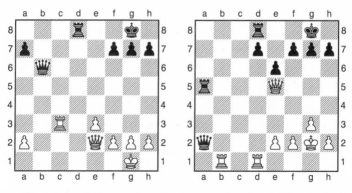

The left-hand diagram is a classic example of exploiting the back rank. Black is to play in the exhibition game O.Bernstein-Capablanca, Moscow 1914. At first sight Black can win by 1...♕b6-b1+ 2 ♕e2-f1 ♖d8-d1, pinning the queen, but this fails because Black has a weak back rank and White can mate by 3 ♖c3-c8+. Capablanca actually played **1...♕b6-b2!**, a brilliant exploitation of *White's* weak back rank. The queen cannot be captured, because 2 ♕e2xb2 runs into 2...♖d8-d1#, while otherwise White's queen and rook are both under fire. White resigned as he has no way to avoid losing a rook; for example, 2 ♖c3-c2 ♕b2-b1+ 3 ♕e2-f1 ♕b1xc2 or 2 ♕e2-e1 ♕b2xc3.

The right-hand diagram is a more complicated example, from the game Crouch-Speelman, Hastings 1992/3. White is a pawn down, and decided to restore material equality by 1 ♖d1xd7. After 1...♖d8-f8 the game ended in a draw. However, White could have won by exploiting Black's weak back rank. The decisive line runs 1 ♖b1-b8! ♖a5-a8 (since 1...♖d8xb8 allows 2 ♕e5xb8#, the only other line is 1...♖d8-f8 2 ♖b8xf8+ ♔g8xf8 3 ♕e5-d6+ ♔f8-e8 4 ♕d6xd7+ ♔e8-f8 5 ♕d7-d8#) 2 ♖d1-a1! and, amazingly, Black cannot avoid losing a queen for a rook; for example, 2...♖d8xb8 3 ♖a1xa2 or 2...♕a2xa1 3 ♖b8xd8+ ♖a8xd8 4 ♕e5xa1. This example shows that back-rank combinations often involve surprising and counter-intuitive moves, and that they are easy to overlook!

Back on page 83, I mentioned that double checks usually arise as part of a mating attack. Here is an example.

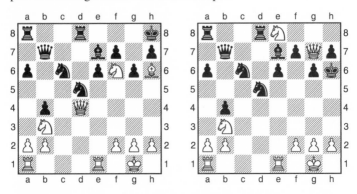

White is to play in the left-hand diagram, and he already has a knight and bishop menacing Black's king. Unfortunately, his queen and knight are both under attack so the discovered checks don't help him. What he needs to do is to give a double check, because this always forces a king move, even if his pieces are under attack. He starts by 1 ♗h6-g7+! (decoying the enemy king) 1...♔h8xg7 2 ♘f6-e8++ ♔g7-h6 (this is forced, owing to 2...♔g7-g8 3 ♕d4-g7# and 2...♔g7-f8 3 ♕d4-h8#) 3 ♕d4-g7+ (*see the right-hand diagram*). White's sacrifice has driven the black king right out into the open, in front of the defensive pawn-wall which would normally shield it. The situation in which a king is chased all over the place by the attacker is normally called a **king-hunt**. In some cases the outcome of a king-hunt can be hard to predict – it often depends on how many attacking pieces are available to harass the king. Here there is no real doubt about the outcome – White's queen and e1-rook are perfectly placed for the attack, and the e8-knight and kingside pawns can join in the fun, too. By contrast, Black's pieces are mostly stuck on the queenside and can play no part because White can operate entirely with checks. Here there are two variations, but the play is similar in either case. After **3...♔h6-g5**, White wins by **4 h2-h4+ ♔g5-g4** (the alternatives are 4...♔g5-f5 5 ♕g7xf7+ ♘d5-f6 6 ♕f7xe6+ ♔f5-f4 7 g2-g3+ ♔f4-f3 8 ♖e1-e3# and 4...♔g5-h5 5 ♕g7xh7+ ♔h5-g4 6 ♖e1-e4+ ♘d5-f4 7 ♖e4xf4+ ♔g4xf4 8 ♕h7xf7+, etc.) **5 ♖e1-e4+ ♘d5-f4 6 ♖e4xf4+ ♔g4xf4 7 ♕g7xf7+ ♔f4-g4 8 ♕f7-f3+ ♔g4xh4 9 ♕f3-f4+ ♔h4-h5 10 ♘e8-g7#**. After **3...♔h6-h5** the finish is **4 ♕g7xh7+ ♔h5-g5** (or 4...♔h5-g4 5 ♖e1-e4+ ♔g4-f5 6 ♕h7-h3+ ♔f5xe4 7 ♕h3-f3+ ♔e4-e5 8 ♖a1-e1+ ♘d5-e3 9 ♖e1xe3#) **5 h2-h4+ ♔g5-g4 6 ♖e1-e4+ ♘d5-f4** (6...♔g4-f5 7 ♕h7xf7+) **7 ♖e4xf4+ ♔g4xf4 8 ♕h7xf7+ ♔f4-g4 9 ♕f7-f3+ ♔g4xh4 10 ♕f3-f4+ ♔h4-h5 11 ♘e8-g7#**. All these lines may seem rather complicated, but I have only given them for completeness. In reality, one hardly needs to calculate every line to be sure that Black's king will be caught.

Next we will see how an attacking position can naturally evolve into one of these standard finishes.

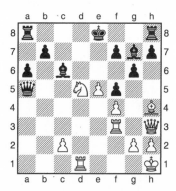

The above diagram is from Nunn-Sutton, Peterborough 1984 (as a testament to the unreliability of some computer data, in one popular database the venue for this game is given as St Petersburg!). White has already sacrificed a pawn in order to attack. In return, all White's pieces are in aggressive positions, while Black's king and rooks are still on their original squares. White's bishop prevents Black castling queenside, but Black still has the option of castling kingside or leaving his king in the centre.

1 ♖f3-d3!

White's first task is to force Black's king to commit itself.

1...0-0

Black cannot afford to wait; for example, 1...♖a8-c8 2 ♘d5-f6+ ♗g7xf6 3 ♗h4xf6 (attacking the h8-rook, and intending ♕h3-h4, followed by ♖d3-d8+) 3...0-0 4 ♕h3-h6 mates.

However, now that Black's king is no longer a mobile target, White finds it easier to press home his attack.

2 ♘d5-e7+ ♔g8-h8 3 ♗h4-f6

White's pieces close in on the black king; the immediate threat is 4 ♕h3-h6. An exchange on f6 will occur sooner or later, but then White has the formation with a pawn on f6 discussed on page 120.

3...♗g7xf6

The only real alternative is 3...h7-h5, but then White wins by 4 ♕h3-h4 ♗c6-e4 (or 4...♗g7xf6 5 ♕h4xf6+ ♔h8-h7 6 ♘e7xf5 g6xf5 7 ♕f6xf5+ ♔h7-h6 8 ♕f5-g5+ ♔h6-h7 9 ♕g5xh5+ ♔h7-g7 10 ♖d3-g3#) 5 ♕h4-g5 ♔h8-h7 6 ♗f6xg7 ♔h7xg7 7 ♖d3-d6, and there is no defence to the threat of 8 ♖d6xg6+ f7xg6 9 ♕g5xg6+ ♔g7-h8 10 ♕g6-h6#.

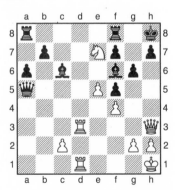

4 ♕h3xh7+!

Even when one of the standard patterns appears on the board, one should always be alert for possible finesses. In the examples we saw earlier, the queen sacrifice on h7 only occurred after White had established his pawn on f6. Here, however, 4 e5xf6 would give Black the chance to defend for the moment by 4...h7-h5. As mentioned on page 79, it is often worth looking to see if it helps to play a sequence of moves in a different order. Here, sacrificing the queen first cuts out Black's ...h7-h5 defence.

4...♚h8xh7 5 e5xf6 1-0

Black resigned as he can only avoid the threat of 6 ♖d3-h3# by 5...♗c6xg2+ 6 ♚h1xg2 ♛a5-d5+, but then he is a piece down with more material to fall soon.

Moving back even further, let's see how to build up an attack from scratch.

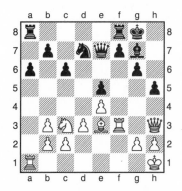

This position is from Nunn-Barua, Hastings 1993/4. It must be emphasized that you should not attempt to build up an attack regardless of the position on the board. There have to be some advantages already present in order to justify starting an attack. In the diagram position, White has a number of small advantages. Each one is not especially significant in itself, but taken together they provide all the preconditions necessary for launching an attack. First of all, the pawn-shield in front of Black's king has been weakened by the advance of the h-pawn, which should really be back on h7. Secondly, White's pieces are more active than Black's; his queen, f3-rook and bishop are well placed for attacking purposes, and the other rook can swing across in one move. Thirdly, Black has no active play himself and so cannot do much to disturb the build-up of White's attack.

1 g2-g4!

The attack starts. Black's protruding pawn on h5 makes it easier for White to whittle away the black king's pawn-cover.

1...h5xg4 2 ♕h3xg4 ♘d7-f6 3 ♕g4-h4

White now has the possibility of ♖f3-h3 which, combined with ♗e3-g5, would give him dangerous threats along the h-file.

3...♕e7-e6 4 ♗e3-c5

A useful move. White gains time, and by controlling f8 he prevents Black's king fleeing from the gathering storm on the kingside.

4...♖f8-e8 5 ♖a1-g1

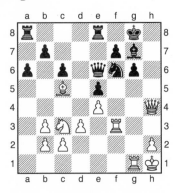

Another piece slides smoothly into an attacking position, while Black has not managed to reinforce his defence at all. Now the only white piece not playing a part in the attack is the knight.

5...♘f6-h5

Black attempts to block the h-file.

6 ♘c3-e2

Intending ♘e2-g3 to challenge the defensive knight on h5. Notice how White does not attempt to push home his attack prematurely. The key to success is to have more pieces attacking than your opponent has defending, so it is essential to move all the reinforcements into position.

6...♖a8-b8

Black cannot really improve his position, but this move reveals his main problem – the a8-rook is too far away to support the kingside.

7 ♘e2-g3 ♘h5xg3+?

Black should have tried to retain this knight by 7...♘h5-f4, when White would have a dangerous attack but no forced win.

8 ♖g1xg3

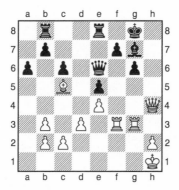

Now all White's pieces are directly attacking Black's king and it is not surprising that the situation is hopeless. The immediate threat is 9 ♖g3-h3 followed by ♕h4-h7#, so Black must drive the enemy bishop back.

8...b7-b6 9 ♗c5-e3 ♕e6-d7 10 ♖g3-h3 ♔g8-f8

Trying to escape from the danger zone, but there is no chance of survival.

11 ♕h4-h7 ♖b8-b7 12 ♕h7xg6

White exploits the f-file pin to register his first material gain.

12...♖e8-e6

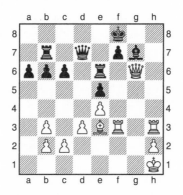

13 ♖h3-h8+!

White finishes with a combination.

13...♗g7xh8 14 ♗e3-h6+ ♔f8-e7 15 ♖f3xf7+ 1-0

Black resigned because after 15...♔e7-d8 16 ♖f7xd7+ ♔d8xd7 17 ♕g6-h7+ ♖e6-e7 18 ♕h7xh8 or 15...♔e7-d6 16 ♖f7xd7+ ♖b7xd7 17 ♗h6-f8+ White ends up with a decisive material advantage.

Attacking play is a fundamental part of chess, but it is also an area that requires a great deal of creativity and inspiration. Even though the finish often falls into one of the familiar patterns, the earlier stages of an attack may be far from easy to play. However, this should not put you off launching an attack when conditions are favourable – the reward for success is often a satisfying and spectacular victory.

Exercises

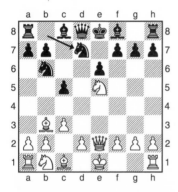

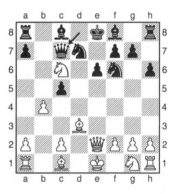

1) In this position taken from the game Magem-Glavina, Saragossa 1994, Black has just played ...♘b8-d7?. How did White use a typical attacking motif to break through?

2) In this position from Gershon-Finkel, Ubeda 1997, Black has just played ...♕d8-c7. How did White break through to the enemy king?

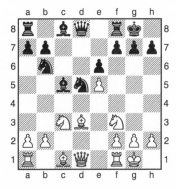

3) This position arose in Groszpeter-Linker, Berlin 1990. How did White (to play) use a sacrifice to set up the standard attacking formation of queen on h5 plus knight on g5?

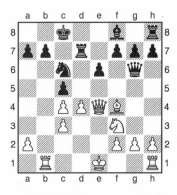

5) It is White to move in this position from Benjamin-Gamboa, Philadelphia 1995. How did he set up a typical bishop and rook mate?

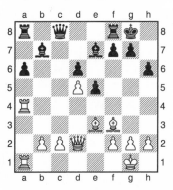

4) In this position from the game Small-Stuart, New Zealand Championship 1985, White has the chance to break through on the kingside. Although the start of White's attack is not difficult, you have to find one tricky move later on.

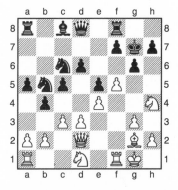

6) It is White to play in this position from Jirovsky-Adamek, Mlada Boleslav 1992. How does White win using one of the standard attacking formations? The first couple of moves are easy, but one further finesse is necessary to break down Black's defence.

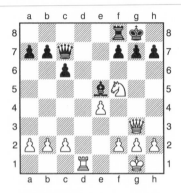

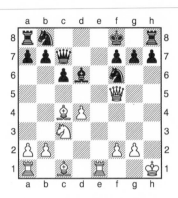

7) White is a pawn up in this position from Capablanca-Fonaroff, New York 1918. However, winning the position based only on the extra pawn would not be easy. However, Capablanca found a short-cut based on Black's back rank. How did he win?

9) This position arose in the game Douven-Zagema, Groningen 1989. White, at the cost of a pawn, has forced Black's king to move and so deprived it of any possibility of castling. How did White (to play) force home his attack?

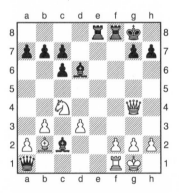

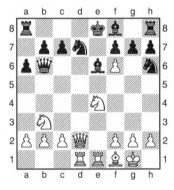

8) This position arose in the game M.Kuijf-Bosboom, Dutch Championship 1991. White has just played ♕e2-g4, attacking Black's queen and threatening ♕g4xg7#. How did Black reply?

10) If a double check is dangerous, what about a *double* double check? How does White (to play) win in the diagram?

Solutions to Exercises

1) Black's last move cut off the c8-bishop's defence of the e6-pawn, and allowed White to exploit the traditional weakness of the f7-square when Black has not castled. After **1 ♘e5xf7** Black resigned. His queen and h8-rook are forked, and if 1...♔e8xf7, then 2 ♕e2xe6#.

2) Once again, the knight on d7 blocking Black's defence of e6 proved the culprit. White forced mate in two with the spectacular queen sacrifice **1 ♕e2xe6+!**. Black resigned as both 1...f7xe6 2 ♗d3-g6# and 1...♗f8-e7 2 ♕e6xe7# are mate.

3) White started his attack by **1 ♗d3xh7+! ♔g8xh7 2 ♘f3-g5+**. Black cannot play 2...♔h7-h6 because White wins his queen by 3 ♘g5xf7++, so the king must move to g8 or g6. In the former case, White reaches his target position and wins by 2...♔h7-g8 3 ♕d1-h5 (threatening 4 ♕h5-h7#) 3...♖f8-e8 4 ♕h5xf7+ ♔g8-h8 5 ♕f7-h5+ ♔h8-g8 6 ♕h5-h7+ ♔g8-f8 7 ♕h7-h8+ ♔f8-e7 8 ♕h8xg7#. Therefore Black played **2...♔h7-g6**, but resigned after **3 ♕d1-c2+ f7-f5** (if 3...♔g6-h5, then 4 ♕c2-h7+ ♔h5-g4 5 ♕h7-h3#) **4 e5xf6+** since 4...♔g6xf6 5 ♘c3-e4+ ♔f6-e7 6 ♕c2xc5+ leaves White material ahead with a crushing attack.

4) The conditions for a kingside attack are relatively favourable. All White's pieces except for the a1-rook are able to take part, while Black only has one bishop defending the kingside. White began with **1 ♗e3xh6 g7xh6 2 ♕d2xh6**, threatening 3 ♖a4-g4+, and therefore forcing **2...f7-f5**. So far, so good, but how does White achieve more than perpetual check with the queen on g6 and h6? The answer is that a further sacrifice is necessary: **3 ♕h6-g6+** (3 ♖a4-g4+ is equally good) **3...♔g8-h8 4 ♖a4-g4!** (opening the line from e4 to h7) **4...f5xg4 5 ♗f3-e4** (Black can only prevent the threatened ♕g6-h7# by giving away several pieces) **5...♖f8-f7 6 ♕g6xf7 ♕c8-g8 7 ♕f7xe7 1-0**. Black is two pawns down, with more losses to come.

5) White played **1 ♕e4xc6+** and Black resigned since 1...b7xc6 is met by 2 ♖b1-b8#, while otherwise White has made off with a piece for nothing.

6) White started with **1 f5-f6+ ♔g7-h8 2 ♕d2-h6**, forcing **2...♖f8-g8**. Now it is natural to try bringing a rook to the h-file, but that isn't possible in this position. Instead White must use his h4-knight to create a mating threat on h7: **3 ♘h4-f3** (heading for g5) **3...♕d8-f8** (the only possible defence; Black tries either to exchange queens or to drive the white queen away from h6; Black can avoid mate by 3...g6-g5 4 ♘f3xg5 ♖g8xg5 5 ♕h6xg5 ♕d8-g8, but at the cost of losing too much material) **4 ♘f3-g5!** (White ignores the threat to his queen) **1-0**. Black resigned as 4...♕f8xh6 allows 5 ♘g5xf7#, while otherwise Black cannot reasonably defend h7.

7) The weakness of Black's back rank is not at all obvious in the diagram, but Capablanca found a spectacular way to exploit it: **1 ♘f5-h6+ ♔g8-h8 2 ♕g3xe5! ♕c7xe5 3 ♘h6xf7+ ♖f8xf7** (or else Black ends up a piece and two pawns down) **4 ♖d1-d8+ 1-0**. It is mate in two more moves.

8) Black managed to get his own mate in first by exploiting White's weak back rank: **1...♕a1xf1+!** and White resigned in anticipation of 2 ♔g1xf1 ♗c2xd3+ 3 ♔f1-g1 ♖e8-e1#.

9) White won with a combination which combines two elements: a weak back rank and the typical bishop + rook mate: **1 ♕f5xf6!** and Black resigned, as 1...g7xf6 2 ♗c1-h6+ ♔f8-g8 3 ♖e1-e8+ ♗d6-f8 4 ♖e8xf8# is the end.

10) In return for the sacrificed piece, White has a formidable array of fire-power lined up against Black's centralized king. However, to make use of this requires imagination and some sacrifices: **1 ♕d2xd7+! ♗e6xd7** (all Black's moves are forced) **2 ♘e4-d6++** (the first double check) **2...♔e8-d8 3 ♖e1-e8+!** (this further sacrifice sets up the second double check) **3...♗d7xe8 4 ♘d6xf7++ ♔d8-c8 5 ♖d1-d8#**.

7 The Phases of the Game

The study of chess is often divided into three parts: opening, middle-game and endgame. We will adopt this system in the current chapter, while bearing in mind that in practice there is rarely a clear dividing line between these phases. Moreover, not every game features all three parts; many games, for example, are decided in the middle-game and never reach the endgame.

The Opening

The **opening** is that part of the game in which both sides bring their forces into play. Initially, the pieces are blocked in behind the pawns and if a player did not move any pawns, he could only play with his knights. Therefore, each player will make some pawn moves with the idea of **developing** his more powerful units. Which pawns should he move? In general, the centre of the board (the squares d4, d5, e4 and e5) is the most useful area to control. There are two main reasons for this. Firstly, as we saw long ago, most pieces control the greatest number of squares when they are in the centre. Thus control and occupation of the centre is a way to enhance the activity of your pieces. Secondly, a piece in the centre can readily switch to the queenside or kingside and so can, directly or indirectly, exert its influence over the whole board. On the other hand, a piece stuck far away on the queen-side will probably have no influence at all on the kingside. If the kingside becomes the key battleground, then the distant piece will be virtually useless.

Thus the pawns which are most often moved in the opening are the d- and e-pawns. Advancing one of these not only helps to control the centre, it also allows development of the queen and a bishop. Ideally, White would probably like to play both d2-d4 and e2-e4. Note that all the comments in this section on opening play apply equally to Black, who should be aiming for ...d7-d5 and/or ...e7-e5. If advancing two pawns is good, perhaps advancing three or more is better? Should White also play c2-c4 and f2-f4? The answer is that it depends on the specific position. There certainly are openings where it is possible to advance three or four pawns in the opening, but there is a danger involved in this. Remember that advancing pawns is not an end in itself, but a means to enable the development of the more powerful pieces. It is easy to become obsessed with pawn moves, and to forget the other pieces. Then there is a danger of falling behind in development, and allowing the opponent to launch an attack while your pieces are still asleep on their original squares. No system of opening play can operate independently of the opponent; if you see he is aiming for quick piece development, then you should do the same.

If you look at games played by grandmasters, you will sometimes find that White does not start with 1 d2-d4 or 1 e2-e4; instead he plays 1 c2-c4, 1 ♘g1-f3 or even some other move. How, you may wonder, does this fit in with what I have been saying above? The answer is that grandmasters are cunning beasts, and starting with 1 c2-c4 or 1 ♘g1-f3 doesn't mean that they aren't aiming at controlling the centre – they are just doing so in a subtle way. Almost certainly, one of those centre pawns is going to advance in the next few moves, but they want to see what their opponent is planning before deciding exactly how to play in the centre. Of course, if the opponent is equally cunning, he can adopt the same non-committal strategy, which is why many modern games are quite hard to explain! However, to begin with I would recommend that you avoid these subtle opening systems; they depend on a knowledge of a wide range of openings, and this can only be acquired over a period of time.

Let's suppose that White has managed to play d4 and e4, allowing the development of both bishops. Which pieces should he bring into play now? More often than not, it is better to develop a knight before a bishop. The reason is that the best square for a bishop is normally not very clear, whereas it is usually more obvious where a knight should be placed. Of course, this is only a rule of thumb and there are many exceptions.

Another major objective of opening play is to castle quickly. This not only safeguards the king by positioning it behind a solid wall of unmoved pawns, but also brings a rook to the centre. The most likely point of contact between the opposing forces is the centre, and it is here that pawn exchanges are most likely to lead to an open file. Therefore, it is usually desirable to position the rooks on the central files.

To summarize, the three key objectives of opening play are:
1) To develop the pieces.
2) To control the centre.
3) To safeguard the king.

The means of achieving these objectives are many and diverse, but if you keep these three principles in mind then you are unlikely to go far wrong.

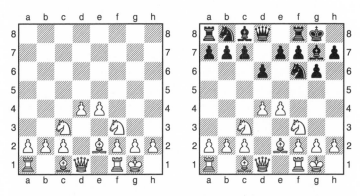

The left-hand diagram shows a typical early piece deployment by White. He has played d2-d4 and e2-e4, and followed up by developing his knights where they have the most influence on the centre. Indeed, the squares d5 and e5 are each controlled twice, once by a knight and once by a pawn. White has developed his bishop to the modest square e2, where it admittedly does not help much in the fight for the centre, but it does allow White to castle immediately. In the diagram he has already done so, and his next move might be ♖f1-e1, or he may look to see if the c1-bishop can be developed to an active square. The right-hand diagram shows a real opening position (from an opening called the Pirc Defence). Black has countered White's set-up by aiming to control the dark squares in the centre, especially the e5-square. His plan is ...♗c8-g4, followed by ...♗g4xf3 and then ...e7-e5, whereby he obtains a foothold in the centre. Because White moves first and so can stake the first claim in the centre, early on Black is often in a position of reacting to White's plans rather than playing actively himself. Only when he has neutralized White's early lead will he look for ways to improve his own position by active play.

The above diagrams obviously present only an idealized portrait of White's ambitions. Black may well adopt a strategy preventing White even getting so far as to play both e2-e4 and d2-d4; in this case White will have to adapt his plans accordingly. Nevertheless, a piece deployment something like the left-hand diagram is available to White in a number of openings.

It is easy to demonstrate the wide range of opening plans available to both sides by considering a simple example. Suppose White plays 1 e2-e4; what can Black play in reply? Of the 20 possible legal moves, no fewer than eight are regularly seen in grandmaster play and two more are played occasionally. In each case, Black intends to challenge White in the centre somehow. Here are these ten moves, with their names and the ideas behind them:

1) 1...c7-c5 is called the Sicilian Defence. Black intends to make it more awkward for White to play d2-d4. Even if White does manage to play d2-d4, then the exchange of Black's c-pawn for White's d-pawn will leave Black with two central pawns against one for White.

2) 1...e7-e5 has no specific name, because it can lead to several different major openings at a later stage. Once again, Black's main aim is to prevent d2-d4.

3) 1...e7-e6 is the French Defence. Black allows 2 d2-d4 by White, but intends to reply 2...d7-d5, establishing a foothold in the centre at d5.

4) 1...c7-c6 is the Caro-Kann Defence. The idea is similar to 1...e7-e6, namely to support ...d7-d5 next move. Playing ...c7-c6 has the advantage of not blocking in the c8-bishop, but the disadvantage of taking the square c6 away from the knight on b8.

5) 1...d7-d6 is the Pirc Defence. Black will probably play ...e7-e5 at some stage, in order to obtain some central control. However, he generally prefers to concentrate on safeguarding his king by ...♘g8-f6, ...g7-g6, ...♗f8-g7 and ...0-0 before taking action in the centre.

6) 1...g7-g6 is called the Modern Defence. Black's aims are rather similar to those in the Pirc Defence, but being committed to the development of the bishop on g7 has both pros and cons.

7) 1...♘g8-f6 is the Alekhine Defence. Black disturbs White's plan to play d2-d4 by simply attacking the e4-pawn.

8) 1...d7-d5 is the Scandinavian Defence. Just as in the Alekhine Defence, Black gives White no time to play d2-d4 because he is immediately attacking the e4-pawn.

9) 1...b7-b6 is Owen's Defence. Black intends to attack the e4-pawn with ...♗c8-b7. However, this opening gives White a fairly free hand in the centre and is not very popular.

10) 1...♘b8-c6 is called the Nimzowitsch Defence. Black will normally play either ...e7-e5 or ...d7-d5 very soon, but first he waits to see if White really intends to play d2-d4. Again, this is a slightly offbeat opening.

To each of these openings, White has a number of possible responses and the repeated branching at each move gives rise to a host of possibilities after only a few moves. In view of this, one might imagine that it would be impossible to study the openings to any great depth. However, this is not so. Many opening lines are inferior and are no longer played, which cuts down the number of branches. Moreover, certain standard lines of play have become accepted as offering fair chances to both sides. The players may use one of these as a short-cut to reach the middlegame without having to expend too much thought on the opening. The literature of chess openings is vast, and whole books can be devoted to one tiny sub-variation. However, studying openings in this detail is only really important at a more advanced level, and for now general principles should suffice.

What Can Go Wrong in the Opening?

Certain mistakes occur time and time again in the opening. Here are the most common:

1) Attacking too soon. As explained in Chapter 6, you should not start an attack without justification. One of the prerequisites for an attack is that you have sufficient firepower available to drive the attack home – an attack that stalls half-way is no good. Pieces on their original squares are of little value in supporting an attack – they have to be developed and in play to be effective. Therefore the basic principle is: **develop your pieces before contemplating an attack**.

2) Repeatedly moving the same piece. Try not to move the same piece again and again in the opening. Best of all is to make sure that **each move is by a different piece**, at least for the first five or six moves. This is the way to get the maximum number of pieces into play as quickly as possible. Obviously, you must not interpret this advice too literally; if your opponent attacks one of your pieces, you may have to move it or lose it. However, as a general guideline it is worth adhering to when you can.

3) Making too many pawn moves. We have already touched on this. The general principle is easy to understand: opening play has to strike a balance between the pawn moves that are necessary to allow the other pieces out, and the developing moves by those other pieces. However, deciding where the balance lies in a particular position is tough even for grandmasters. As a rule of thumb, if you make more than three pawn moves in the first eight moves, then you should take care!

4) Not castling. Since much of the early action is likely to take place in the centre, it is usually important to whisk the king out of the line of fire by castling. If you delay castling for too long, the escalating struggle may envelop the king before you have a chance to castle, so **don't delay castling**.

5) Exposing pieces to attack. Another balance which has to be struck during the opening is that between moving the pieces forward to active positions and advancing them so far that they can be attacked by enemy pieces and driven back with loss of time. When a more valuable piece is attacked by a less valuable piece, it usually has to move. If this happens repeatedly, then a great deal of time can be wasted. You are normally safe with pawns, because there is nothing less valuable than a pawn, but you should already take care with minor pieces. If a minor piece is attacked by a pawn, then it normally has to move away.

The left-hand diagram on the following page is a case in point. This position arises after the moves **1 e2-e4 c7-c5 2 ♘b1-c3 ♘b8-c6**. If White now ignored point 2 above and played 3 ♘c3-d5, then Black

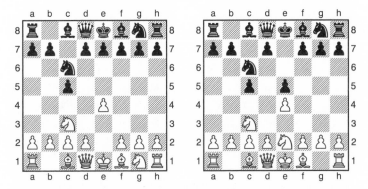

could reply 3...e7-e6, attacking the knight, which would then have to retreat ignominiously to c3 or e3.

In the right-hand diagram, the further moves **3 ♘g1-e2 e7-e5** have been played. In contrast to the previous position, 4 ♘c3-d5 is now a very reasonable move. Black's c- and e-pawns have advanced too far to attack the knight on d5, so the knight is secure against pawn attack. White can then continue his development by ♘e2-c3, ♗f1-c4 and 0-0. This would bring his king into safety, and then the queenside pieces could come out by d2-d3, etc.

The rooks generally take more time to develop than the other pieces, since everything else has to be cleared out of the way before the rooks can occupy the central files. This development normally occurs in the middlegame rather than the opening, so the problem of exposing a rook to attack at an early stage rarely arises.

The queen is the worst piece to expose to attack, because it can be chased around by any enemy piece except for the opposing queen. **You should not move your queen into the opposing half of the board in the opening**, except if you have a very good reason. The likelihood of the queen being trapped is quite high, and even if it manages to escape with a whole skin, considerable time will have been lost. Once again, if you look at the games of famous players such as Fischer and Kasparov, you will find that they occasionally break this rule, especially in a notorious opening line called the Poisoned Pawn Variation. Well, probably they can get away with it, but many lesser grandmasters have lost embarrassingly quickly trying to do the same thing.

The Middlegame

A typical middlegame scenario develops as follows: at the end of the opening both sides have more or less completed the development of their forces, but so far there has been no major contact between the two armies, except possibly in the centre. Now the middlegame starts. Both sides manoeuvre, trying to improve the position of their forces and to weaken the position of the enemy forces. They must be on the lookout for possible ways to win material, or to start a successful attack on the enemy king. Of course, there are many other possible scenarios. Sometimes the forces engage in battle at a very early stage, before development is complete, while in other cases a blocked pawn-structure leads to slow-motion manoeuvring and the main battle occurs far later.

The middlegame is perhaps the part of chess in which differences in skill are most apparent. To some extent, opening play is a matter of careful study, but in the middlegame there are fewer guidelines and the player's skill is the dominant factor. However, this does not mean that there is no point studying the middlegame. While natural talent cannot be taught, there are many useful skills that can be.

We have already dealt with two of the most important middlegame topics: winning material by tactical means, and playing for a direct attack on the opposing king. In these situations, concrete calculation is essential – the typical "If I go there, then he goes there, then I take that..." type of thought with which all chess-players are familiar. However, what do you do if neither of these options is available? The answer is that you have to employ a different type of thinking which depends less on move-by-move calculation and more on the creation and execution of plans spanning several moves. The objective of the plan can be any favourable change in the position, but the following are typical:

1) To improve the position of one's own pieces, for example by occupying a crucial square.

2) To gain control of a key line, such as an open file or an important diagonal.

3) To drive an enemy piece from a strong post.

4) To improve the preconditions for an attack.

We will look at examples of each of these objectives.

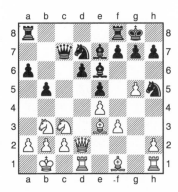

This position is from Nunn-Hanreck, Sutton 1980. Black has just played ...b7-b5 and White has to formulate a plan. I decided to exploit a potential weakness of Black's last move, namely that Black's b-pawn no longer controls the square c6. At the moment White exerts no control over this square, but within a few moves the situation has changed completely.

1 ♘c3-d5

The first step in the plan. Black is forced to exchange this knight, as his queen and e7-bishop are attacked. If 1...♕c7-d8, then 2 ♘d5xe7+ ♕d8xe7 3 ♕d2xd6 wins a pawn.

1...♗e6xd5 2 e4xd5

Taking back with the pawn gives White control of c6. However, this control would be of little value if there were no way to bring a piece to c6. Fortunately, there is a ready-made route available: ♘b3-a5-c6.

2...♖f8-b8?

Black makes no effort to counteract White's plan and indeed even makes matters worse, because this rook will be attacked when the knight arrives on c6. There were two reasonable ways to meet White's plan. 2...♗e7-d8 would have prevented White's intended manoeuvre, forcing him to switch to another plan. Alternatively, Black could have played 2...f7-f5, ignoring White's plan but aiming for active counterplay on the kingside. This choice is typical when it comes to countering your opponent's ambitions: you can either give priority to blocking his ideas, or you can give him a free hand and use the time to further your own plans.

3 ♘b3-a5 ♗e7-d8 4 ♘a5-c6 ♖b8-b7

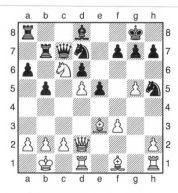

White's plan has succeeded. He has planted a knight on c6, while Black has not improved his position at all. The only chance to get rid of the knight is to play ...♘d7-b8, but it is not so easy to realize this idea. Whether Black could have defended better in the rest of the game is beside the point; White's plan has given him a clear advantage.

5 ♗f1-h3 (the threat is 6 ♗h3-g4) **5...g7-g6** (5...♘d7-b8 6 ♗h3-g4 g7-g6 7 ♗g4xh5 g6xh5 8 ♘c6xd8 ♕c7xd8 9 ♕d2-b4 followed by ♕b4-h4 wins the h5-pawn) **6 ♗h3-g4 ♘h5-g7 7 f3-f4 e5xf4 8 ♗e3xf4 ♘d7-b8 9 ♕d2-g2** (it's still not so easy to get rid of the c6-knight!) **9...♗d8-e7 10 ♘c6xe7+** (White changes tack; his powerful knight disappears, but in return Black's queenside pieces are imprisoned) **10...♕c7xe7 11 ♕g2-g3 ♖b7-b6 12 ♖h1-e1 ♕e7-f8 13 ♖d1-d3** (threatening ♖d3-c3-c8; at the moment the knight on b8 cannot move) **13...a6-a5** (freeing the knight to meet ♖d3-c3 by ...♘b8-a6, but now White reveals a second point behind his previous move) **14 ♕g3-h4** (intending ♖d3-h3, with a deadly attack against h7) **14...♘b8-a6 15 ♖d3-h3 ♘g7-h5 16 ♗g4xh5 g6xh5** (Black's position is a total wreck and the rest is just mopping up) **17 ♗f4-e3 ♖b6-b7 18 ♗e3-d4 ♖a8-e8 19 ♖e1-d1 ♕f8-e7 20 ♕h4xh5 ♕e7-e4 21 ♖h3-e3 ♕e4xe3 22 ♗d4xe3 ♖e8xe3 23 ♕h5-h6 ♖b7-d7? 24 g5-g6 1-0**

The position on the following page arose in the game Ree-Cornelis, Siegen Olympiad 1970. White is to play. At first sight his advantage is very slight. True, he has the two bishops, but the light-squared

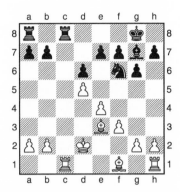

bishop is impeded by the many white pawns on light squares. Moreover, the single open file will make it hard for White to avoid the exchange of all the rooks, which will further reduce his advantage. The main plus-point is that his bishop on e3 is attacking the a7-pawn; sooner or later Black will be forced to deal with this threat.

White found an excellent plan, which enabled him to gain control of the open c-file.

1 ♖c1xc8+ ♖a8xc8 2 g2-g3

Note that 2 ♗e3xa7 is bad because 2...♖c8-a8 regains the pawn with an improved position for Black.

The intention of the move played is to develop the bishop at h3. The h3-c8 diagonal is clear of white pawns, so the bishop will have an unobstructed field of operation. After ♗f1-h3 Black's rook will have to decide whether to stay on the first rank (to meet ♗e3xa7 by playing the rook to a8) or to concede the d-file.

2...♘f6-d7

Black tries to have the best of both worlds and keep his rook on the c-file while at the same time preventing ♗e3xa7.

3 ♗f1-h3 ♖c8-c7

Now 4 ♗e3xa7 is bad because of 4...b7-b6 5 ♗h3xd7 ♖c7xa7, when the d7-bishop, the a2-pawn and the b2-pawn are all under attack.

4 ♗h3xd7! ♖c7xd7 5 b2-b3

White removes the b2-pawn from attack and now genuinely threatens to take on a7. Black must spend a tempo meeting this threat.

5...a7-a6 6 ♖h1-c1

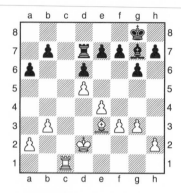

White's plan has succeeded; he controls the only open file on the board. This confers a large advantage, because his rook threatens to penetrate to either c7 or c8, and Black cannot defend both squares. In contrast, Black's rook is doomed to a permanently passive role. The phase of the game of interest to us is over; suffice to say that, at the very least, Black has an extremely difficult position. In the game White increased his advantage and won convincingly.

6...h7-h5 7 ♖c1-c8+ ♔g8-h7 8 ♗e3-b6 (sealing in the enemy rook) **8...f7-f5 9 ♔d2-d3 f5xe4+ 10 ♔d3xe4 ♗g7-f6 11 a2-a4 ♔h7-g7 12 f3-f4 ♔g7-f7 13 f4-f5 ♗f6-e5 14 b3-b4 ♔f7-f6 15 f5xg6 ♔f6xg6 16 b4-b5 a6xb5 17 a4xb5 ♔g6-f6 18 ♗b6-e3 e7-e6** (at long last Black manages to free his rook, but the price is high: there is no way to save the h5-pawn) **19 ♖c8-h8 e6xd5+ 20 ♔e4xd5 ♔f6-g6 21 ♖h8-h6+** and Black resigned. After 21...♔g6-g7 22 ♖h6xh5, White not only has an extra pawn but his pieces (especially his king) are still far more active than their black counterparts.

This position on the following page arose (with White to play) in Nunn-Dickenson, Islington 1981. Black has spent considerable time developing his pieces to active squares on the queenside. Altogether, five moves were required to occupy b4 and c5, namely ...♕d8-b6, ...♕b6-b4, ...♘b8-d7, ...♘d7-c5 and ...a7-a5 (the last was required to prevent White playing b2-b4, kicking the knight away). However, this was a double-edged plan. Although the queen and knight appear well placed at the moment, if White can force them to retreat then Black will have spent all this time for nothing. The fact that one of

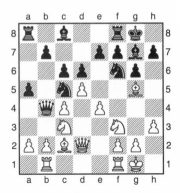

the pieces involved is the enemy queen is already a promising sign. We know that it can often be unwise to develop the queen early on, because it can so easily be chased around by lesser pieces.

White must first of all deal with Black's threat ...♛b4xc4 before he can consider how to expel Black's pieces.

1 ♕d2-e2

Now White threatens 2 a2-a3 ♛b4-b6 3 b2-b4, driving Black's pieces away, so Black's next move is more or less forced.

1...a5-a4

So as to meet 2 a2-a3 by 2...♛b4-a5, when White can no longer drive the knight away by b2-b4 because of the *en passant* capture.

White now formulates a plan spanning four moves to drive Black back on the queenside.

2 ♗g5-d2

The first step. White threatens to trap the queen by 3 ♘c3-b5 or 3 ♘c3xa4, so Black has to retreat.

2...♕b4-b6 3 b2-b4

The second step. If Black is to avoid an immediate knight retreat, then he has to take *en passant*.

3...a4xb3 4 a2xb3

Now that White has eliminated Black's a-pawn, there is nothing Black can do to prevent b3-b4 next move.

4...♘f6-h5 5 b3-b4 ♘c5-d7 6 ♗d2-e3 ♕b6-c7 7 ♘f3-d4

We can see that White's plan has been a success. The queen and knight have retreated to Black's second rank, and there is nothing left of the queenside pressure Black spent so long preparing. White has a solid, well-supported pawn-centre and all his pieces are in play. Black is cramped and his c8-bishop has no moves at all.

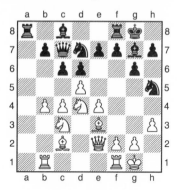

7...♘h5-f4

A little trick. If 8 ♗e3xf4, then 8...♗g7xd4 and the exchange of knights relieves a little of the congestion in Black's position.

8 ♕e2-d2

Now the f4-knight is genuinely attacked.

8...e7-e5 9 d5xe6 ♘f4xe6 10 ♘d4-e2

White avoids the exchange of minor pieces, which would help Black resolve the traffic-jam in his position. We will see the same strategy later in Example Game 4 (see page 175).

10...♘d7-e5

Black strives to activate his pieces, and again attacks the c4-pawn. However, these pinprick attacks are not supported by the rest of Black's army and so pose no real danger to White.

11 ♗c2-b3

The c4-pawn is defended, and White is ready to drive the e5-knight back by f2-f4. It is the same story as before: Black cannot maintain his pieces in good positions.

11...c6-c5

Desperation. Black hopes to secure the square d4 for his pieces, but this move has the serious defect of allowing White to occupy d5.

12 f2-f4 ♘e5-c6 13 f4-f5 ♗g7xc3

Exchanging this important defensive bishop exposes Black's king, but there was little choice as 13...♘e6-d4 loses to 14 f5-f6 ♗g7-h8 15 ♘c3-d5 ♕c7-d8 16 b4-b5, followed by ♘d5-e7+.

14 ♘e2xc3 ♘e6-d4 15 ♘c3-d5 ♕c7-d8 16 ♗e3xd4 ♘c6xd4 17 ♕d2-h6 1-0

Black resigned as there is little he can do to prevent White setting up the typical attacking formation with queen on h6 and pawn on f6 (see page 120). The immediate threat is 18 e4-e5! d6xe5 19 ♘d5-e7+! ♔g8-h8 (or 19...♕d8xe7 20 f5-f6, winning the queen) 20 f5xg6, and if 17...♖a8-a3 then 18 ♗b3-d1, followed by 19 f5-f6 ♘d4-e6 20 ♗d1-g4, eliminating the knight on e6 and mating on g7.

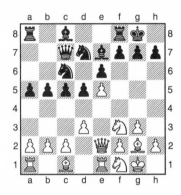

This position arose, with White to play, in Ciocaltea-Kozma, Sochi 1963. It is noteworthy not only for the way White built up his attack, but also for the spectacular and brilliant finish.

In the diagram, White has the makings of a kingside attack, since Black has no defensive minor pieces in front of his king. However, the attack will not break through easily; Black's defensive pawn-wall is unbroken, and some of White's queenside pieces are still on their original squares. What White needs is a plan that improves the pre-conditions for an attack without committing him irrevocably to a do-or-die onslaught.

1 h2-h4

White hits on an excellent plan: he pushes his pawn from h2 all the way up to h6. Then Black will have to play ...g6 or else allow an exchange of pawns. In either case his pawn-wall will be weakened. The advance of the h-pawn involves a low level of commitment; no sacrifice is involved, and White has not decentralized any of his pieces.

1...b5-b4 2 ♗c1-f4

White takes time out to improve his development, but he could also have played 2 h4-h5 straight away.

2...♗c8-a6 3 ♘f1-e3 ♖a8-a7?

Black does not seem to realize the danger, and plays far too slowly.

4 h4-h5 ♖f8-c8 5 h5-h6 g7-g6

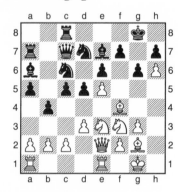

Thanks to White's excellent choice of plan, his attack looks far more promising than it did in the previous diagram. We saw earlier (page 120) how a friendly pawn in the vicinity of the enemy king poses a permanent danger; here White only needs to get his queen to g7 to mate.

6 ♘e3xd5!

White's attacking chances have improved to the point where he can commit himself further without undue risk. This sacrifice opens a path to Black's king.

6...e6xd5 7 e5-e6 ♕c7-d8 8 e6xf7+!

This is much stronger than 8 e6xd7. White is interested in mate, not in regaining the sacrificed piece.

8...♔g8-h8

If 8...♔g8xf7, then 9 ♕e2-e6+ ♔f7-f8 10 ♘f3-g5! (threatening 11 ♕e6-f7#) 10...♗e7xg5 11 ♗f4-d6+ ♘c6-e7 12 ♗g2xd5, followed by mate.

9 ♘f3-e5!

The attack continues in spectacular style. The following variations are worth looking at closely; note how, time and time again, the attack depends on the h6-pawn for its success.

9...♘d7-f6

After 9...♘c6xe5 White has a beautiful win by 10 ♕e2xe5+! ♗e7-f6 (10...♘d7xe5 11 ♗f4xe5+ ♗e7-f6 12 ♗e5xf6+ ♕d8xf6 13 ♖e1-e8+ ♖c8xe8 14 f7xe8♕+ mates, while after 10...♘d7-f6 11 ♗f4-g5 Black cannot meet the threat of 12 ♗e5xf6+ ♗e7xf6 13 ♕e5xf6+! ♕d8xf6 14 ♖e1-e8+) 11 ♕e5-e8+ ♘d7-f8 12 ♖e1-e6! (threatening 13 ♕e8xd8 followed by ♖e6xf6, so the bishop must move) 12...♗f6xb2 13 ♗f4-e5+!! (a fantastic finish) 13...♗b2xe5 14 ♖e6xg6 (threatening mate on g8) 14...h7xg6 15 ♕e8xe5+ followed by mate on g7 (that h6-pawn again!).

10 ♘e5xc6 ♖c8xc6 11 ♕e2-e5

White's threats are just too strong.

11...♖c6-d6 12 ♗g2xd5!

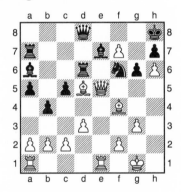

12...♗a6-b5

Or 12...♖d6xd5 13 ♕e5xf6+! ♗e7xf6 14 ♖e1-e8+.

13 ♗f4-g5 ♗b5-c6 14 ♗d5xc6 1-0

As after 14...♖d6xc6 we have the familiar conclusion 15 ♗g5xf6+ ♖c6xf6 16 ♕e5xf6+ ♗e7xf6 17 ♖e1-e8+ followed by mate.

What Can Go Wrong in the Middlegame?

The short answer is – almost anything! Just as the middlegame offers the greatest scope for originality and creativity, so it also offers the greatest scope for things to go wrong. However, the main points to bear in mind are simply the reverse of the positive advice given above.

1) Stay alert for tactical opportunities, both for yourself and for your opponent. Watch out for the warning signals mentioned on page 91.

2) Don't play without a plan. This is one of the most common errors. Almost any position is capable of improvement, given time. Work out how to activate your pieces or gain control of important squares and lines. At the same time, you should keep an eye on what your opponent is doing. Your own plans do not function in a vacuum; they can be affected by your opponent's actions. It may be advisable to take time out to counter his plans. However, if in doubt it is usually better to get on with what you are doing than to fall into a permanently passive frame of mind in which you only think about how to block your opponent.

3) Keep your king safe. Do not unnecessarily weaken the pawn-cover in front of your king. If your opponent seems to be building up for an attack against your king, check that you have some defensive pieces in place.

The Endgame

If the game has not been decided earlier, it eventually enters the endgame. The dividing line is hard to define, but as pieces disappear from the board the character of the game gradually changes. We will assume that the struggle is still in the balance; if one side already has a decisive advantage, then the endgame may be no more than a mopping-up operation leading to the promotion of a pawn and victory.

In a typical endgame, both sides will have a king and some pawns, and probably one or two heavier pieces each. As the more powerful pieces disappear, the role of the kings and pawns becomes more significant. The key objective in the endgame is the promotion of a pawn, thereby obtaining a material advantage sufficient for victory. One concept is of great importance: that of a **passed pawn**. A passed pawn is one which can no longer be prevented from promoting by an enemy pawn.

The diagram on the following page illustrates this idea. White's pawn on a4 cannot advance towards promotion, because it is blocked by the enemy pawn on a5. Therefore, this is not a passed pawn. The pawn on b2 is also not a passed pawn, because it is restrained by the

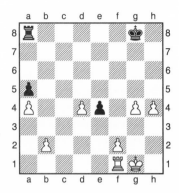

pawn on a5; if White were to play b2-b4, Black could reply ...a5xb4. The pawn on d4 is passed; although Black has a pawn on the adjacent e-file, it is too far up the board to stop the d4-pawn advancing. The pawns on e4 and f2 restrain each other, so neither of these is passed. Note that f2-f4 can be met by an *en passant* capture. The pawns on g4 and h4 are both passed, and form a pair of **connected passed pawns**, i.e. two passed pawns on adjacent files.

Normally, possession of a passed pawn is an advantage. The opponent has to prevent the pawn advancing, and this usually ties up an enemy piece, such as a knight or bishop, which could be better used on some other task. Having a piece occupied may not be a great burden when there are many pieces on the board, but it becomes more and more of a handicap as the forces thin out. Thus passed pawns become progressively more important as the game proceeds, and in an endgame they are often the deciding factor.

Two connected passed pawns are especially dangerous. A passed pawn is usually stopped by putting a piece directly in front of it. If there is a second passed pawn on an adjacent file this may not be possible, because the blockading square is controlled by the second pawn. Thus two connected passed pawns should be advanced, so far as possible, in line abreast, in order to drive away any pieces in their path.

While a passed pawn is usually an asset, it has to be properly supported. There is no point in pushing a pawn into the enemy half of the board, only to see it encircled and captured. This brings us to the second important point about endgames: the use of the king. The middlegame is a dangerous environment for a king; powerful pieces are flying around the board, ready to exploit any chink in the king's armour. During this phase of the game, the king has to be carefully protected. As the more powerful pieces are exchanged off, the danger to the king becomes less and less, until finally the danger of mate becomes minimal, and the king may safely venture into battle. Indeed, not only *can* the king enter the battle, it *should* do so. Despite the king's limited range and slow-motion gait, its omnidirectional power makes it an effective weapon. It is particularly dangerous if it can penetrate amongst the enemy pawns, and is fully capable of digesting a whole row of pawns, if given the chance. The king is also very good at supporting friendly passed pawns.

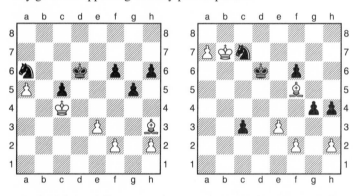

In the left-hand diagram, which arose in Karpeshov-Shaposhnikov, USSR Championship selection tournament, Roslavl 1989, White has a passed pawn on a5. At the moment the pawn is blocked by the enemy knight, but White can dislodge the knight with his king. Black, it is true, also has a passed pawn, but it is not supported by his king. The game continued **1 ♔c4-b5 ♘a6-c7+ 2 ♔b5-b6 c5-c4** (Black tries to gain counterplay with his own passed pawn) **3 ♗h3-f5** (White uses his bishop to block the enemy pawn) **3...c4-c3 4 a5-a6** (White's own pawn advances; Black cannot stop it because White's king is in a position to dislodge the knight whenever it tries to occupy a square, such as a8, in front of the pawn) **4...g5-g4** (Black can only wait) **5 a6-a7 h6-h5 6 ♔b6-b7 h5-h4** (*see the right-hand diagram*) **7 ♗f5-c2** (White could win the knight by promoting his pawn, but then the black king could run up to b2, supporting his own passed pawn; White aims to promote his pawn *without* allowing Black to give up his knight for it) **7...♔d6-d7 8 ♗c2-a4+ ♔d7-d6 9 e3-e4 1-0**. Black resigned because his only reasonable move is 9...h4-h3, but after 10 ♗a4-c2 ♔d6-d7 11 ♗c2-d1 ♔d7-d6 12 ♗d1-a4 Black has no reasonable move at all.

What Can Go Wrong in the Endgame?

While it is in general desirable to play actively with your king in the endgame, this doesn't mean that you should completely ignore possible dangers.

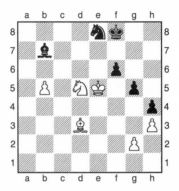

In the diagram above, from Short-Beliavsky, Linares 1992, Black has just played ...f7-f6+. White would have had good winning chances after the simple 1 ♘d5xf6, but instead he decided to use his king actively by **1 ♔e5-e6??**. The reply **1...♗b7-c8#** showed that even a leading grandmaster can have a blind spot concerning king safety in the endgame.

It is also quite easy to overlook tactics involving the creation or promotion of passed pawns.

In the left-hand diagram overleaf, from Sarkar-Nur, USA Junior Championship, Washington 1996, Black played **1...g7-g6** only to be surprised by **2 g4-g5!**. This move ensures that White obtains a passed h-pawn; for example, after 2...h6xg5 3 h5-h6 or 2...g6xh5 3 g5xh6 Black cannot catch the pawn with his king. Black could only try **2...♔d6-e7 3 g5xh6 ♔e7-f6**, but after **4 h6-h7 ♔f6-g7 5 h5xg6 f7xg6 6 c4-c5 ♔g7xh7 7 b4-b5 ♔h7-g7 8 c5-c6 b7xc6 9 b5xc6** Black resigned, since now the passed c-pawn is unstoppable.

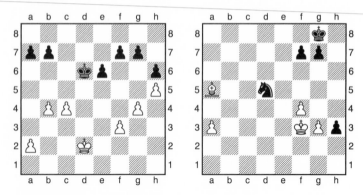

The right-hand diagram above is from Medina-Tal, Palma de Mallorca 1966. It is Black to play and although he already has a passed h-pawn, it seems to pose little danger because 1...h3-h2 can be met by 2 ♔f3-g2. However, Black played **1...♘d5-e3!** and White resigned, because now that the square g2 is covered, White cannot stop the pawn promoting.

Exercises

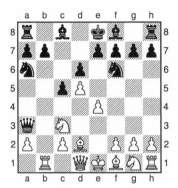

1) This position arose in the game Zambor-Kundrik, Slovakian Team Championship 1997/8 after **1 d2-d4 ᐃg8-f6 2 ᐃc1-g5 c7-c5 3 d4-d5 ᐃd8-b6 4 ᐃb1-c3 ᐃb6xb2 5 ᐃg5-d2 ᐃb8-a6 6 ᐃa1-b1 ᐃb2-a3 7 e2-e4 d7-d6**. How did White punish Black's early queen excursion?

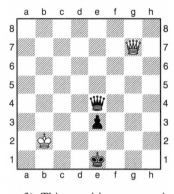

3) This position arose in Batuev-Simagin, Riga 1954. In order to win, Black must promote his pawn, so he continued 1...e3-e2. Was this a good move?

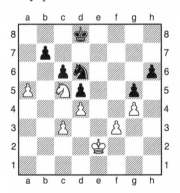

2) In this position from Ciolac-Dobosz, Goetzis 1996, how did White (to play) win?

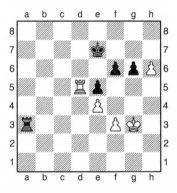

4) How can White (to play) make use of his passed pawn on h6?

Solutions to Exercises

1) White won Black's queen by **8 ♘c3-b5 ♕a3xa2** (8...♕a3-a4 loses to 9 ♘b5xd6+ e7xd6 10 ♗f1-b5+) **9 ♖b1-a1** and now 9...♕a2-b2 is met by 10 ♗d2-c3. In the game Black preferred **9...♕a2xa1**, but resigned after **10 ♕d1xa1 ♘f6xe4 11 ♕a1-a4 ♘e4xd2 12 ♘b5xd6++ ♔e8-d8 13 ♘d6xf7+ ♔d8-c7 14 ♗f1xa6 1-0**.

2) White won with a surprising knight sacrifice: **1 ♘c5xb7+!**. If now 1...♘d6xb7, then 2 a5-a6 and Black cannot prevent the pawn promoting. The game continued **1...♔d8-c7 2 ♘b7xd6 ♔c7xd6** (Black's position is hopeless as he has lost the vital b-pawn for nothing) **3 f3-f4! 1-0**. After 3...g5xf4 4 ♔e2-f3 ♔d6-c7 5 ♔f3xf4 ♔c7-b7 6 ♔f4-f5 ♔b7-a6 7 ♔f5-g6 ♔a6xa5 8 ♔g6xh6 White promotes well ahead of Black, and wins easily.

3) It certainly wasn't. Black had forgotten about the possibility of mate, even in an ending. After **1...e3-e2**, White played **2 ♕g7-g1+ ♔e1-d2 3 ♕g1-c1+ ♔d2-d3 4 ♕c1-c3#**. Black should have played 1...♕e4-b4+ 2 ♔b2-c2 ♕b4-c4+ 3 ♔c2-b2 ♔e1-d2, when he can win although it still requires considerable care. However, even if Black could not find the route to a win, he certainly shouldn't have lost!

4) White can force the promotion of his h-pawn by **1 ♖d5-d8!**, when Black cannot prevent 2 h6-h7 and 3 h7-h8♕. The resulting ending with queen against rook and pawn is a comfortable win for White. 1 h6-h7 is inferior, as Black can reply 1...♖a3-a8 followed by ...♖a8-h8.

8 Chess Psychology

All sports contain a psychological element. Everybody knows of cases such as the golf player who enters the last round six shots ahead and then collapses, or the tennis player who fails to win a match point and then, despite still being well ahead, falls apart and loses several games in a row. Probably you can think of examples from your own favourite sport. As chess is a mental game, psychological factors are even more important than in a physical sport. The tennis player may find that his reflexes carry him through a period of mental turmoil, but if your brain is not functioning properly during a chess game, then you are likely to be in trouble.

Chess is particularly tough on the mental frailties to which everybody is prone. In most jobs you can get away with the occasional mistake; it may be spotted and corrected later, or it may be accepted that the occasional error is inevitable. However, if you make a mistake in chess, you may be punished for it, not next week or next month, but in a matter of seconds. Moreover, if you make a mistake in tennis then it's just one point that's gone – undesirable, perhaps, but usually far from decisive. If you make one serious error in chess then the game's over and you can go home.

Many of the common psychological errors in chess are bound up with the excitement of playing. Those who do not play chess will not appreciate this point, but if you have got this far in the book then you will probably appreciate the immense thrill of playing chess. The effort of keeping a poker face while having just set a devilish trap, the stomach-churning fear of having overlooked something, the thrill of making a spectacular sacrifice – of course, the excitement is part of the pleasure of chess, but one should try not to let it get out of control and cause unnecessary blunders.

The first typical error is not noticing your opponent's threats. It is easy to become so wrapped up in your own plans, ideas and threats that you overlook what your opponent is up to.

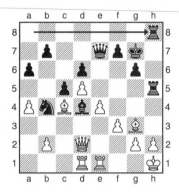

This position arose with White to play in S.Fischer-Heinz, 2nd Bundesliga 1992/3. White is a solid pawn up and undoubtedly stands to win by arranging the advance of his central pawns. Eager to get on with the job, White played **1 f3-f4??** but after **1...♖h5xh2+** he had to resign, as 2 ♗g3xh2 ♖h8xh2+ 3 ♔h1xh2 ♛e7-h4# is mate. White was evidently thinking only of how to convert his advantage into a win and simply overlooked the threat behind Black's last move. The doubled rooks on the h-file are potentially dangerous, and White should have taken great care to make sure that Black could not use them in a surprise tactic. Had White been more alert, he would have played 1 h2-h3!, which nullifies Black's threat and prepares the central advance. It is worth noting that even if Black manages to threaten a sacrifice on h3, White can always play ♗c4-f1 to rule it out for certain.

The error of not noticing your opponent's threat is especially common when you have a winning position. It is easy to allow your mind to drift and you start thinking about what you are going to do when the game is finished. Nasty surprises occur more frequently when your mind is wandering. **The game isn't over until your opponent has actually resigned**.

A second common error is falling into a trap. Suppose your opponent leaves a piece to be taken. It looks like a blunder! This is the time to look carefully for possible danger before snapping off the piece, but it is amazing how many players are unable to control their instinctive response. Just remember: your opponent cannot take the move back once he has played it, so **you don't lose anything by taking care**. If it really is a blunder, all well and good; if it's a trap, then by spotting it in time you may save yourself a painful experience.

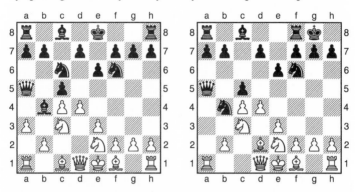

The left-hand diagram arises after the moves **1 d2-d4 ♘g8-f6 2 c2-c4 e7-e6 3 ♘b1-c3 ♗f8-b4 4 e2-e3 c7-c5 5 ♘g1-e2 ♘b8-c6 6 a2-a3 ♕d8-a5**. Black's last move indirectly defends the bishop on b4 by pinning the a3-pawn against the undefended rook on a1. I once saw the following sequence of events from this position: White played **7 ♗c1-d2**, defending the rook on a1 and so 'genuinely' threatening to play a3xb4. Black replied **7...0-0**, ignoring the threat. White was unable to believe his eyes and without a moment's hesitation snapped off the bishop by **8 a3xb4**. After **8...♘c6xb4** (*see right-hand diagram*) White realized that he had fallen into a trap. Black is threatening 9...♘b4-d3#, and after White deals with this by playing, for example, 9 ♘e2-f4, Black continues 9...♕a5xa1 10 ♕d1xa1 ♘b4-c2+ and ends up winning a rook for a bishop. Had White kept his head, then he might have taken a closer look at the position after 7...0-0 and spotted the trap. He might then have realized that instead of the losing move 8 a3xb4??, White can win a piece by playing 8 d4-d5!. In fact, Black's seventh move was a blunder which could have been exploited, but thanks to White's impetuous reaction Black got away with it.

You should always operate on the assumption that your opponent will spot any traps you set. If you have two ways of achieving the same objective, one of which sets a trap and one of which does not, then by all means set the trap – who knows, you have to be lucky sometime! But you should not play a move that has a trap as its only purpose. In the likely event that your opponent sees through your ruse, the best you can hope for is to lose a move for nothing. More likely, as in the example above, the setting of the trap itself compromises your position.

Over-confidence is a common failing in everyday life, and so its appearance at the chessboard is no surprise. It can manifest itself in various ways; a typical example is not taking an opponent seriously because you have beaten him (or her) several times before. The basic rule here is: **every opponent is dangerous**. Take every game seriously; the small girl you are facing today might be a leading grandmaster in years to come.

The opposite error is that of fearing the opponent. Even if your opponent is club champion (or worse) and will probably beat you nine times out of ten, today might be the tenth time! When facing a stronger opponent, remember that every player, even the world champion, makes mistakes. Your job is to be ready to grab any chances that come your way. So stay alert, play your normal game, and hope for the best.

One could extend this list of psychological failings at the chessboard, but you shouldn't become obsessed with self-analysis. A person who is, for example, generally impulsive will also be impulsive at the chessboard. While it is important to be aware of the problems this can cause, you should not waste too much time on the near-impossible task of reforming your own character.

9 Example Games

While it is convenient to treat many chess ideas in isolation, it is also important to see how these ideas fit into the overall context of a complete game. The four games in this chapter contain, in their different phases, many of the ideas that we have covered in earlier chapters. Here we see how these ideas can be linked together in a practical game.

Game 1
M. Al Modiahki – Tin Htun Zaw
Yangon (Myanmar) 1999

For our first example, we return to the game given on page 56 to examine in more detail how White won so quickly.

1 e2-e4 g7-g6

As we saw on page 139, this opening is called the Modern Defence. It is a subtle opening in which Black delays central action until he sees more of White's intentions. The danger is that this delay may allow White to build up such a formidable central position that Black's central counterplay never gets going.

2 d2-d4 ♗f8-g7 3 ♘b1-c3 d7-d6 4 ♘g1-f3

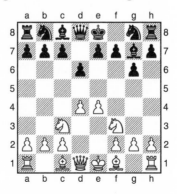

White contents himself with straightforward classical development along the lines of the diagrams on page 137.

4...♘b8-d7?!

This is a poor move, but for a rather subtle reason. From the purely positional point of view there is nothing wrong with it; in this opening Black typically plays either ...c5 or ...e5 to challenge White's centre and this knight move appears to be a flexible way of preparing either of these moves. Indeed, if White were now to play the quiet 5 ♗f1-e2, Black would escape unscathed from his dubious opening experiment. In order to win, it is not enough for your opponent to play bad moves; you must also find the correct way to exploit his mistakes.

Black should have given priority to bringing his king into safety by 4...♘g8-f6 followed by 5...0-0.

5 ♗f1-c4!

White pinpoints the flaw in Black's last move. We noted the weakness of the square f7 in the early stages of the game on page 116. Black's previous move both blocks in his queen and weakens his hold on the e6-square. White's reply threatens a deadly combination: 6 ♗c4xf7+! ♚e8xf7 7 ♘f3-g5+ ♚f7-f6 (or else 8 ♘g5-e6 wins the queen) 8 ♕d1-f3#. This is virtually identical to the combination given on page 117. Black now has to spend a move dealing with White's threat, and once again he is unable to make progress towards castling.

5...c7-c5

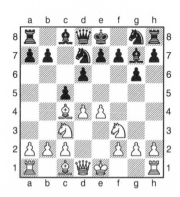

Black meets the threat by giving his queen an escape-route.

6 ♘f3-g5!

This is a very strong move. Sacrificing on f7 immediately is not at all clear; for example, after 6 ♗c4xf7+ ♔e8xf7 7 ♘f3-g5+ ♔f7-e8 8 ♘g5-e6 ♕d8-a5 (making use of the escape-route) 9 ♘e6xg7+ ♔e8-f7 (White's problem is that his knight is trapped) 10 ♘g7-h5 g6xh5 11 ♕d1xh5+ ♔f7-f8 White only has two pawns for the piece.

6...♘g8-h6

Black has no good way to meet the threat to f7. After 6...e7-e6 White sacrifices on e6 instead: 7 ♗c4xe6! f7xe6 8 ♘g5xe6 ♕d8-a5 (8...♕d8-e7 9 ♘c3-d5 ♕e7xe6 10 ♘d5-c7+ ♔e8-e7 11 ♘c7xe6 ♔e7xe6 12 d4xc5 is hopeless for Black – he is material down and his king is fatally exposed) 9 ♘e6xg7+ ♔e8-f7 10 ♘g7-h5 g6xh5 11 ♕d1xh5+ (here White already has three pawns for the piece) 11...♔f7-f8 12 ♗c1-h6+ ♘g8xh6 13 ♕h5xh6+ ♔f8-f7 14 0-0-0 and White should win – material is equal, but Black's king is hopelessly exposed in the centre.

7 ♗c4xf7+! ♘h6xf7 8 ♘g5-e6

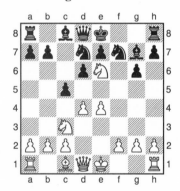

8...♕d8-b6

Here the escape-route is of little help to Black. He could have lasted slightly longer after 8...♕d8-a5, but against a grandmaster it would have made no difference to the eventual result of the game.

9 ♘e6xg7+ ♔e8-f8

In this position, Black's knight is blocking f7, so he cannot even trap the white knight.

10 ♘g7-e6+ 1-0

Why did Black resign? Because after 10...♔f8-g8 11 ♘c3-d5, White both attacks the queen and threatens 12 ♘d5xe7#. Black is unable to meet both threats; for example, 11...♕b6-a5+ 12 b2-b4 doesn't help. If instead 10...♔f8-e8, then 11 ♘c3-d5 followed by ♘d5-c7+ is similar. In every case Black loses his queen.

Lessons from this game:

1) You should only play a complex, modern opening if you know what you are doing.

2) Beware the f7-square (f2-square for White) before castling.

3) Even strong players have off-days, so don't be intimidated by your opponent.

Game 2
Rublevsky – Onishchuk
Moscow Olympiad 1994

1 e2-e4 e7-e5 2 ♘g1-f3 ♘b8-c6 3 ♘b1-c3 ♘g8-f6

This opening goes by the self-explanatory name of 'The Four Knights'.

4 d2-d4 ♗f8-b4

Black complicates the struggle by ignoring White's attack on the e5-pawn. By pinning the knight on c3, he sets up his own attack against the white pawn on e4. 4...e5xd4 5 ♘f3xd4 ♗f8-b4 is a simpler and safer continuation.

5 ♘f3xe5

White calls Black's bluff and simply lops off the pawn he was attacking.

5...♕d8-e7?!

This does regain the pawn White has captured, but the resulting position favours White. Black should have accepted the challenge with 5...♘f6xe4; after 6 ♕d1-g4 ferocious complications arise. This line is a case in which the opening phase is cut short, and a turbulent middlegame starts while most of the pieces are still on their original squares!

6 ♕d1-d3

White must return the pawn as 6 ♘e5xc6 is met by 6...♕e7xe4+. Playing an early queen move always requires careful thought, to see if the queen can be readily attacked by enemy pieces. Here there are three reasons justifying White's choice:

1) The queen is relatively safe from attack on d3.

2) It will help White to castle quickly on the queenside.

3) There is no reasonable alternative. 6 ♗f1-d3 is bad in view of 6...♘c6xd4, which leaves the knight on e5 under fire.

The move played defends the e4-pawn, so that now White is genuinely threatening 7 ♘e5xc6.

6...♘c6xe5 7 d4xe5 ♕e7xe5 8 ♗c1-d2 0-0 9 0-0-0

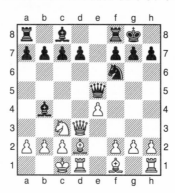

Material equality has been restored, and both sides have castled. Situations such as this, in which the players have castled on opposite sides of the board, tend to lead to attacking play by both sides. If both sides have castled on the kingside, then White (say) will be restricted in his attacking ideas because his own king will obstruct his attacking build-up. Moreover, he will be reluctant to use his pawns to attack the enemy king, as their advance would expose his own king. However, in the diagram position White can attack on the kingside without any such fears.

9...d7-d6 10 f2-f4

White increases his control of the centre with gain of time, because Black's queen must move.

10...♕e5-e7

A key moment in the game. White would like to start a kingside attack, but first he must develop his remaining pieces. At the same time he must cope with the threat to his e4-pawn by ...♗b4xc3 followed by ...♘f6xe4 or ...♕e7xe4. The plan White now adopts provides an efficient solution to both problems.

11 ♖d1-e1!

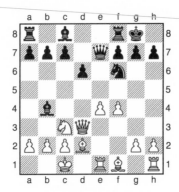

An excellent move. This defends the e4-pawn, freeing the queen to move to g3. This in turn clears the way for ♗f1-d3, after which the h1-rook can move to f1. In only four moves, White will have completed his development smoothly, and his pieces will be well placed for attacking purposes. The rooks, in particular, will be lined up behind mobile pawns which can advance to break open the pawn-wall defending Black's king.

The continuation provides a good example of how the correct choice of plan can effectively decide a game. Four moves from now White has a really dangerous attacking build-up, while Black, who flounders around without a plan, hasn't achieved anything constructive.

11...♖f8-e8 12 ♕d3-g3 c7-c6?!

It is probably slightly better to play 12...♗c8-d7 followed by ...♗d7-c6. This serves the same purpose as the move played (keeping White's knight out of d5) but also develops a piece.

Note that Black cannot win a pawn by 12...♗b4xc3 13 ♗d2xc3 ♘f6xe4 because of 14 ♕g3xg7#.

13 ♗f1-d3 ♘f6-d7 14 a2-a3 ♗b4-a5 15 ♖h1-f1

It is obvious that White has very good prospects on the kingside. All his pieces are available for the attack, while Black has no minor pieces defending the kingside. Nevertheless, White correctly brings all his pieces into play before committing himself to the attack – there is no risk in making sure that the odds are stacked as heavily as possible in his favour.

15...♗a5-c7 16 f4-f5

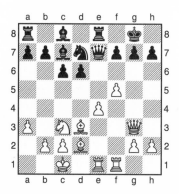

The attack starts!

16...♔g8-h8

This allows a shattering breakthrough, but there was no satisfactory move. If Black tries to block the pawn with 16...f7-f6, then 17 ♗d3-c4+ ♔g8-h8 18 ♕g3-h4, followed by ♖e1-e3-h3, gives White a huge attack.

17 f5-f6!

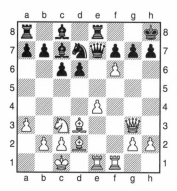

Ripping a hole in Black's defences.

17...g7xf6

The alternative was 17...♘d7xf6, but then 18 e4-e5! d6xe5 19 ♗d2-g5 catches Black in a nasty pin. White will increase the pressure by ♕g3-h4, with threats to both f6 and h7, and it seems very unlikely that Black can defend.

18 e4-e5!

White conducts the attack with great energy. A second pawn is invested to open lines for the rook on e1 and especially the bishop on d3.

18...f6xe5

The other captures lead to a similar conclusion, e.g. 18...♘d7xe5 19 ♗d3xh7 ♔h8xh7 20 ♖f1-f4 or 18...d6xe5 19 ♗d3xh7 ♔h8xh7 20 ♖f1-f5, and White wins in both cases.

19 ♗d3xh7!

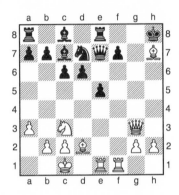

Now the black king is stripped bare. 19...♔h8xh7 loses to 20 ♖e1-e4 followed by ♖e4-h4+. However, declining the sacrifice does not help Black. A king can rarely survive in the middlegame without some sort of defensive cover, and here Black's king has been abandoned by both pieces and pawns.

19...d6-d5 20 ♗h7-f5

Black's situation is hopeless. He is a pawn up, but his king stands naked while the white pieces close in for the kill.

20...f7-f6 21 ♕g3-h4+ ♔h8-g8 22 ♖f1-f3 e5-e4 23 ♘c3xe4 1-0

Black resigned as 23...d5xe4 24 ♖e1xe4 wins easily; for example, 24...♕e7-f7 25 ♖e4xe8+ ♕f7xe8 26 ♕h4-h7+ ♔g8-f8 27 ♗d2-h6#.

Lessons from this game:

1) It is essential to have a constructive plan.

2) Bring as many pieces as possible into play before starting an attack.

3) Once you have committed yourself to an attack, continue as energetically as possible.

Game 3
Ionescu – Conquest
Bucharest 1999

1 ♘g1-f3 c7-c5 2 c2-c4 ♘b8-c6 3 d2-d4 c5xd4 4 ♘f3xd4 e7-e6 5 ♘b1-c3 ♘g8-f6

Once again, we see the 'knights before bishops' principle in operation.

6 g2-g3

The point of White's opening is to obtain a grip on the square d5. The pawn on c4 and knight on c3 already control this square; White intends ♗f1-g2 to bring another piece to bear. Black must somehow interfere with this plan, or else he will find it hard to act in the centre.

6...♕d8-b6

The first disturbance. The d4-knight is attacked and White must retreat it.

7 ♘d4-b3 ♘c6-e5

Now the c4-pawn is threatened. These attacks may look like mere pinpricks, because they are easy enough to meet, but Black's play is more subtle than it might appear.

8 e2-e4 ♗f8-b4

And now it's the turn of the e4-pawn!

9 ♕d1-e2

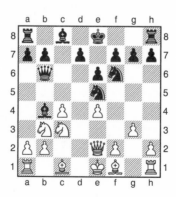

White has countered all the threats and is ready to continue his development by ♗f1-g2 and 0-0.

9...d7-d6 10 f2-f4

However, once again White has to postpone his intended ♗f1-g2 because 10 ♗f1-g2 ♛b6-c7 awkwardly attacks the c4-pawn. White solves this problem in the simplest possible way: he first drives the e5-knight back, and only then plays ♗f1-g2. However, playing f2-f4 opens the diagonal from b6 to g1, and this may make it harder for White to castle kingside. This is really the point of Black's play; if White could simply drive Black's pieces back and complete his development, then he would have a definite advantage, but he cannot achieve this without making some sort of concession.

10...♘e5-c6 11 ♗f1-g2?

The obvious move, but it turns out to be bad. White should have played 11 ♗c1-e3, when 11...♗b4xc3+ 12 b2xc3 ♛b6-c7 13 ♗f1-g2 is roughly equal. Perhaps White believed that Black could not prevent ♗c1-e3 followed by 0-0, but it turns out that this belief is mistaken.

11...e6-e5!

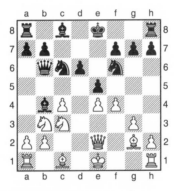

A good move. Black prepares to meet ♗c1-e3 by ...♘c6-d4.

12 ♗c1-d2

White has to change tack. 12 ♗c1-e3 ♘c6-d4! is actually very unpleasant for White, since 13 ♛e2-d3 ♘d4-c2+ 14 ♛d3xc2 ♛b6xe3+ more or less forces 15 ♔e1-f1, when White has lost the right to castle.

12...0-0 13 f4-f5

Relatively the best. With White's king in the centre, he certainly does not want Black opening up the e-file by ...e5xf4. After 13 ♘c3-d5? ♘f6xd5 14 c4xd5 ♗b4xd2+ 15 ♛e2xd2 ♘c6-b4! or 13 ♘c3-b5?

e5xf4 14 g3xf4 ♖f8-e8 15 ♗d2xb4 ♘c6xb4 16 0-0-0 d6-d5! Black
has a large advantage.

13...♗c8-d7 14 g3-g4?

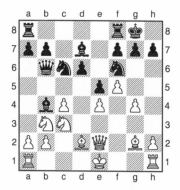

White decides to launch a kingside attack. However, the contrast
with the previous game could hardly be more acute. Far from having
all his pieces in play, White's king and both rooks are still on their
original squares. Indeed, Black is ahead in piece development, because he has already castled and so can bring his rooks into play immediately.

White should have played 14 ♕e2-d3 which, by controlling d4,
threatens to play ♗d2-e3.

14...♘c6-d4

Now that White has really committed himself to an attack, Black
plays to open up the position and start a counterattack.

15 ♘b3xd4?!

Things go from bad to worse. The natural reply would be 15
♕e2-d3, but thanks to White's previous move this is impossible, as
the queen must defend the g4-pawn. White should have at least tried
15 ♕e2-d1, although one can understand his reluctance to put a piece
back on its original square.

15...e5xd4 16 ♘c3-d5 ♘f6xd5 17 c4xd5 d4-d3!

The contrast between the king positions shows how misguided
White's 'attacking' 14th move was. Black's king is safely lodged behind an unbroken wall of pawns, while White's king is stuck in the
centre and has been totally deserted by its pawns – the nearest one is
three squares away. With this move, Black gains time to press home

his attack before White can plug any of the gaping holes in his position.

18 ♕e2xd3 ♗d7-b5

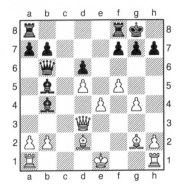

19 ♕d3-f3

There is nothing better, since 19 ♕d3-b3 ♗b4xd2+ 20 ♔e1xd2 ♕b6-f2+ and 19 ♕d3-c2 ♕b6-e3+ are totally hopeless.

19...♗b4xd2+ 20 ♔e1xd2 ♕b6-d4+ 21 ♔d2-e1

21 ♔d2-c1 ♖a8-c8+ leads to a quick mate, so White's king must return.

21...♕d4xb2 22 ♖a1-d1 ♖a8-c8

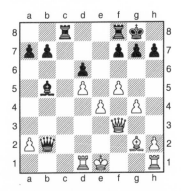

0-1

White resigned as there is no real answer to Black's threat of 23...♖c8-c2 followed by 24...♖c2-e2+ or 24...♕b2-b4+. If 23 ♗g2-f1, then 23...♗b5-a4 wins material with a continuing attack.

Lessons from this game:

1) It is very risky to leave your king in the centre.

2) You should not start an attack which you are unable to support properly.

3) If you make mistakes 1 and 2 simultaneously, your punishment is likely to be severe.

Game 4
Nunn – Rind
Manchester 1980

The previous three games might have given you the idea that complex tactical struggles are the norm in tournament chess. In fact, quiet strategic games are more common. The former are often published because they are more interesting than the latter, but mastery of quiet positions is a great point-winner.

This is a typical positional game; there are no tactics until right at the end.

1 e2-e4 c7-c5 2 ♘g1-f3 ♘b8-c6 3 d2-d4 c5xd4 4 ♘f3xd4 g7-g6

Once again we have a popular contemporary opening, called the 'Accelerated Dragon' (this sounds fearsome enough, but believe it or not there is even a 'Hyper-Accelerated Dragon'). Black intends ...♗f8-g7 in order to increase the pressure against d4.

5 c2-c4

This is White's main antidote to the Accelerated Dragon. His pawns on c4 and e4 exert a firm grip on the central square d5, which makes it difficult to Black to undertake any active play in the centre (rather as White was trying to achieve in the previous game). Much of the game revolves around the two players' competing strategies: Black tries to control d4 while White aims to secure d5.

At one time White's strategy was held to be a virtual refutation of the Accelerated Dragon – some old books talk about it as if it were almost a forced win for White. Chess theory advances, and we now know that Black has reasonable chances and White cannot hope for more than a slight advantage.

5...♘g8-f6 6 ♘b1-c3 d7-d6 7 ♘d4-c2

This retreating move undoubtedly looks rather odd (and I would probably not play it today). The point is that White controls more space: he has two pawns on the fourth rank, while Black has no pawn more advanced than the third rank. Therefore, Black has less room in which to manoeuvre and his pieces may end up tripping over each other in the confined space. Exchanging pieces would help to relieve this congestion, and therefore I decided to side-step the possible exchange of knights. The defect, of course, is that the retreat costs White time. In chess, a move is very rarely entirely positive. Almost every reasonable move has both pros and cons, and the skill is in deciding where the balance lies.

7...&f8-g7 8 &f1-e2 &f6-d7

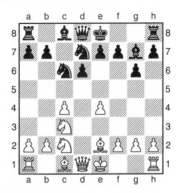

A good idea. Black unmasks his g7-bishop and intends to plant this knight on c5, where it attacks the e4-pawn. If White allows it, Black will double White's pawns by ...&g7xc3+.

9 &c1-d2

White decides to spend a move meeting Black's threat.

9...&d7-c5

Playing the knight to c5 directly allows White to kick it away by playing b2-b4. Black doesn't especially mind this, as the knight can drop back to e6, where it reinforces his control of d4. However, it was also perfectly reasonable to try to keep the knight on c5; for example, after 9...0-0 10 0-0 a7-a5, followed by ...&d7-c5, the position is roughly equal.

10 b2-b4 &c5-e6

Black cannot try to win the e4-pawn by 10...&g7xc3, because after 11 &d2xc3 the rook on h8 is attacked.

11 &a1-c1

White takes care to relieve the awkward pin of the c3-knight.
11...0-0 12 0-0

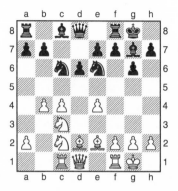

This is a critical position in that both sides have achieved their immediate aims – White controls d5 and Black controls d4. However, if White is given time to play ♘c3-d5 and ♗d2-e3, then he will be able to contest Black's grip on d4. Therefore, Black cannot afford to play quietly and must take active measures straight away.

12...f7-f5?

Black decides to attack White's centre, and remove one of the pawns exerting a grip on d5. However, this turns out to be the wrong plan. The reason is that White's hold on d5 is so strong that it cannot really be broken by this or indeed any other measure. Thus Black should have put his full energy into consolidating his own control of d4, so as to counterbalance White's asset. The best way to do this was by 12...a7-a5 13 a2-a3 a5xb4 14 a3xb4 (the removal of the a-pawns has favoured Black, as he has a rook on the open file while White does not) 14...♘e6-d4 15 ♘c2xd4 ♘c6xd4 16 ♗d2-e3 e7-e5. Now the knight on d4 is secure. White can eliminate it by the exchange ♗e3xd4, but after ...e5xd4 Black has active pieces. An important point to note is that if White plays 17 ♗e3xd4 e5xd4 18 ♘c3-d5, then Black can exchange off White's dangerous knight by ...♗c8-e6 and ...♗e6xd5. In the game, a similar pawn-structure arises, but with the light-squared bishops already exchanged. This makes a huge difference because then Black has no means to eliminate a white knight on d5.

13 e4xf5 g6xf5

Also after 13...♖f8xf5 14 ♗e2-d3 ♖f5-f8 15 ♗d3-e4 White retains his grip on d5.

14 f2-f4!

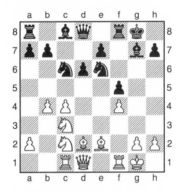

An absolutely vital move. If Black is allowed to play ...f5-f4, then the square e5 becomes a secure base for his pieces, and after ...♘c6-e5 he would have the makings of a dangerous kingside attack. After the move played, an interesting situation exists in the centre. Black still has both his central pawns, while White's have disappeared. One might think that the pawn-structure would therefore favour Black, but this is not so as Black's central pawns cannot move without creating weaknesses. For example, if Black plays ...e7-e6 or ...e7-e5, then the d6-pawn is weak as it cannot be defended by a pawn, and Black has no hope of pushing his d-pawn while White retains his hold on d5.

This position is easier to play for White than for Black, because White has a clear-cut plan. If all the minor pieces were exchanged, then White's advantage would be very clear. He could put his rooks and queen on the d- and e-files, and exert pressure against e7 or, if the e7-pawn advances, against d6. Thus White has only to play for exchanges, whereas it is harder to come up with a good plan for Black. White's immediate threat is 15 ♘c3-d5, followed by ♗d2-e3, when Black loses his control of d4.

14...♘e6-d4

Black decides on the same plan as recommended in the note to his 12th move, but the preliminary ...f7-f5 makes it far less effective now than it was then.

15 ②c2xd4 ②c6xd4 16 ♗d2-e3

Better than 16 ♗e2-d3 ♗c8-e6, followed by ...♖a8-c8, when the c4-pawn comes under attack.

16...e7-e5?

Now this is not good. 16...②d4xe2+ 17 ♕d1xe2 ♗c8-d7 was a better chance, but still somewhat favourable for White.

17 ♗e2-f3

Heading for d5. White should not go in for the greedy 17 ♗e3xd4 e5xd4 18 ②c3-b5, when 18...a7-a6 19 ②b5xd4 ♕d8-b6 20 c4-c5 ♕b6xb4 leads to unclear complications.

17...♗c8-e6

After 17...②d4xf3+ 18 ♕d1xf3 Black has little to show for his weak d6-pawn.

18 ♗f3-d5!

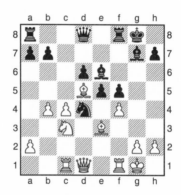

This exchanges off the one black piece which can contest White's control of d5. Then White's knight can settle there in absolute safety.

18...♕d8-d7 19 ♗d5xe6+ ♕d7xe6 20 ②c3-d5

Threatening 21 ②d5-c7.

20...♖f8-f7 21 ♗e3xd4 e5xd4 22 ♖f1-e1 ♕e6-d7 23 ♕d1-d3

This position is extremely favourable for White – indeed, I believe that with good play it is winning for White. Why is this, and why is the situation so different from the note to Black's 12th move?

The foundation of White's advantage is the difference in the power of the two minor pieces. White's knight on d5 is enormously strong, controlling several squares in Black's camp. Best of all, it can never be dislodged or exchanged. Black's bishop, on the other hand,

can only stare glumly at the blockading pawn on d4. Black also has
problems because the f5-pawn is weak. A side-effect of all this is
that White will gain control of the open e-file; Black cannot double
rooks because the knight controls e7, and in any case the exchange of
all the rooks would probably cost Black the f5-pawn.

There are two key differences between this position and that arising in the note to Black's 12th move. The most important is that the
light-squared bishops have been exchanged, which prevents Black
playing ...♗e6xd5 and forcing White to recapture with a pawn.
When your plan involves occupying a central outpost with a piece, it
is almost always a failure for the key square to be occupied by one of
your own pawns. That is what has happened here with regard to the
d4-square; it is blocked by a black pawn, so not only does Black lose
the possibility of establishing a piece on d4, the pawn even obstructs
Black's bishop. The second difference is that the move ...f7-f5 has
damaged Black's kingside pawn-structure and opened the e-file,
which will fall into White's hands.

23...♖a8-c8

After 23...♖a8-e8 24 ♖e1-e2 White will gain control of the e-file
in any case.

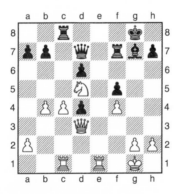

24 b4-b5

A safety-first move. The only way Black could dislodge the d5-
knight would be to get rid of the c4-pawn by ...b7-b5; by playing b4-
b5, White rules out even this unlikely possibility.

**24...♖c8-f8 25 ♖c1-c2 a7-a6 26 ♖c2-e2 ♔g8-h8 27 a2-a4 a6xb5
28 a4xb5**

It is also not bad to play 28 c4xb5, aiming to create a passed pawn on the queenside, but White prefers to keep his knight absolutely secure.

28...♕d7-d8 29 h2-h3

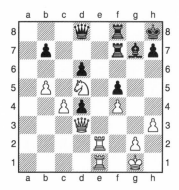

There is no doubt that White has a winning position. Possible plans include attacking the d6-pawn by ♖e2-e6 and ♕d3-a3, or aiming to swap off a pair of rooks by ♖e2-e7. However, there is a basic principle when you have a winning position and your opponent is completely passive: **do not hurry**. You should do all you can to tidy up any loose ends in your position before instituting the decisive action. Here White creates a secure refuge for his king on h2. If, for example, all the rooks were exchanged and Black managed to give a queen check on White's back rank, it would be nice to have the safe spot h2 ready for the king. Of course, this may never happen but White loses nothing by being ready for it.

29...♕d8-a5 30 ♖e2-e6 ♕a5-d8 31 ♕d3-a3

White tries the first of the above-mentioned plans. Black cannot defend his weak d6-pawn so he sacrifices it.

31...♕d8-h4 32 ♖e1-e2

32 ♖e6xd6 was impossible because of 32...♕h4xe1+, while 32 ♕a3xd6 d4-d3 gives Black some counterplay based on his passed d-pawn and the possibility of ...♗g7-d4+. In fact, careful analysis shows that White can defuse this counterplay by 33 ♕d6-c5, but in over-the-board play it is hard to be sure of this. In general, if it is possible to win without allowing counterplay, then you should do so. **Do not take risks when you are winning**.

After the move played, White is really threatening 33 ♖e6xd6.

32...♖f8-g8

Black prevents 33 ♖e6xd6 due to 33...♗g7-f8 pinning the rook. White therefore decides to abandon the plan of winning the d6-pawn and instead goes for the second plan mentioned in the note to White's 29th move. White has lost nothing by toying with the first plan, since Black has been unable to improve his position.

33 ♕a3-d3

Once again d6 is attacked, so Black has to retreat.

33...♕h4-d8 34 ♖e6-e7

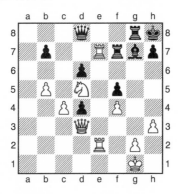

This is a better plan. White wins without allowing any counterplay.

34...♖g8-f8 35 ♖e2-e6

Making room for ♕d3-e2.

35...♖f7xe7

Black concedes the seventh rank to White's rook, but this could not have been prevented in any case; for example, 35...♕d8-c8 36 ♔g1-h2 ♕c8-d8 37 ♖e7xf7 ♖f8xf7 38 ♕d3-e2 (threatening ♖e6-e8+) 38...♖f7-f8 39 ♖e6-e7.

36 ♖e6xe7 ♕d8-c8

Now Black's pieces have the additional responsibility of defending the b7-pawn.

37 ♔g1-h2

Another tidying-up move. On h2 the king cannot even be checked.

37...♖f8-e8

A desperate move, but continued passive defence would not hold out for long, as White's queen can infiltrate: 37...♕c8-b8 38 ♕d3-g3

♖f8-g8 39 ♕g3-g5 ♕b8-f8 (or 39...♕b8-c8 40 ♘d5-f6) 40 ♕g5-h5 d4-d3 41 ♖e7-f7 ♕f8-d8 42 ♘d5-e7, with the deadly threats of 43 ♘e7-g6# and 43 ♘e7xf5.

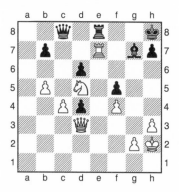

38 ♖e7xg7

White concludes the game with a small combination. There is nothing wrong with this method, but, had he wished, White could also have won by 38 ♖e7-c7, which forces the queen to abandon either the b7-pawn or the f5-pawn.

38...♚h8xg7 39 ♕d3xd4+ ♚g7-f8

39...♚g7-f7 offers slightly more resistance, but 40 ♕d4-f6+ ♚f7-g8 41 ♕f6xd6 (threatening both 42 ♘d5-f6+ and 42 ♘d5-e7+) 41...♕c8xc4 42 ♘d5-f6+ ♚g8-f7 43 ♘f6xe8 ♚f7xe8 44 ♕d6-b8+ wins the b7-pawn with check. Then White would be two pawns up.

40 ♕d4-h8+ ♚f8-f7 41 ♕h8xh7+ ♚f7-f8

41...♚f7-e6 42 ♕h7-g6+ ♚e6-d7 43 ♘d5-b6+ wins the queen.

42 ♘d5-f6 ♖e8-d8

42...♖e8-e1 43 ♕h7-g8+ again wins Black's queen.

43 ♕h7-g8+ ♚f8-e7 44 ♘f6-d5+ ♚e7-d7 45 ♕g8-f7# (1-0)

Lessons from this game:

1) An invulnerable piece in the centre of the board is a formidable asset.

2) If there is only one open file on the board, gaining control of it is very important.

3) If you are winning, there is no need to rush. Take as few risks as possible in converting your advantage into victory.

10 Improving Your Chess

Having read this book, you will probably be wondering how to improve your game further. There are endless possibilities for playing and reading about chess, and the only limitation is the amount of time you are able to devote to it.

In order to improve, you need to combine over-the-board experience with studying. Finding suitable opponents is always a problem when you are starting out. Playing against human opponents face-to-face is the most enjoyable form of chess, and it is worth finding out if you have a local chess club, or if there is a chess club at your place of work or study. However, games between players of greatly different ability are usually not very interesting, and you may find that some opponents at a chess club are too good for you ... at the moment! Some clubs are not especially friendly towards beginners, but equally some are very welcoming and do their best to point you in the direction of someone your own strength.

It is of course possible to play against a computer, but current computer programs are capable of beating the world champion when run at full power, so before buying one you should make sure that it has a range of levels suitable for different standards of opponents.

If you are unable to visit a chess club, it is possible to play chess online, which is increasingly popular. There are several venues for online chess, both free and fee-based. Not surprisingly, the fee-based systems are generally better designed and more active. The two main fee-based chess servers are the Internet Chess Club (www.chessclub.com) and www.playchess.com, which is the online chess service of the ChessBase company. If you buy a ChessBase playing program, such as *Fritz*, you generally get a year's subscription to playchess.com included. Both ICC and playchess.com operate a rating system, which makes it easy to find opponents of approximately your own strength. Other services, such as online coaching, are also available. Both sites offer a free trial (currently 7 days at ICC and 30 days at playchess.com) so you can see what they have to offer. Most online chess is **blitz**, in which each player has either three or five minutes for the whole game. Those with the fastest mice may even choose to play **bullet**, which involves having just one minute each for the game. If you prefer to play a more sedate game, then the online chess world is probably not for you and you would be better off going to a nearby chess club or entering a local tournament.

One of the wonders of the Internet is the possibility of following the world's top tournaments live online. Most of the leading tournaments have a basic live broadcast of the games, but both ICC and playchess.com offer live commentary for all the important events, and players can gather online to discuss the games as they are being played. Following the commentary and trying to guess the players' moves in advance is both entertaining and a good way to improve your chess.

You can also play chess online for free, for example at the Free Internet Chess Server (http://www.freechess.org/) or even at Yahoo! Chess. A search with Google will turn up other possibilities, but the success of any online chess club depends on achieving a critical mass of players and this only occurs at the most popular sites.

If you are a parent whose child wants to play chess online, a couple of words of warning are in order. Online chess servers generally include a 'chat' facility. Although in the vast majority of cases this is used only for friendly conversation, abusive language does sometimes occur. Moreover, as in any case in which children are active online, parents should take care that inappropriate liaisons are not developed.

While on the subject of the Internet, there are a lot of chess resources available on the Web. These include chess news, club notice-boards, games collections and discussion groups. Unfortunately, information on the Internet tends to be a moving target; just when you publish a list of addresses, half of them change. However, two of the main sites for chess news have been around for a long time and are unlikely to change: www.chessbase.com and www.chessvibes.com. Otherwise, it's probably best to use a search engine.

Whenever possible, you should record your games for later study. If you have been playing on a computer, this usually involves just saving the game in a database. If you have been playing at a club or in a tournament, then it is a good idea to enter the game later into a computer from your score-sheet (see page 188). By looking at your games afterwards, you can see where you played well and where you played badly, and work out which part of your game needs the most attention. If you have a playing program, then you should have it watching while you replay the game. Look at the computer's ideas; you will be amazed how many times the machine spots something you didn't even consider during the game.

Competitive Chess

If you start playing competitive chess, then you will have to get used to a whole series of rules and conventions governing play.

Chess clocks have been employed for timing competitive games since the mid-19th century. One 'chess clock' is really two clocks, which register the total thinking time for each player. After making a move, you press a lever or button on the top of the clock, which stops your clock and starts your opponent's. These days, the traditional mechanical clocks have largely been replaced by electronic clocks, which are more accurate.

The time-limit varies greatly from event to event and, surprisingly, there is no universal standard even for top-level international events. Exceeding your time allocation results in automatic loss of the game, so remember to press your clock after making a move! A sporting opponent might point out that you have forgotten to press your clock, but he is under no obligation to do so. There are three main categories of time-limit; from slowest to fastest, these are tournament, rapid and blitz. The last is regarded as more for fun than for 'serious' chess, and most competitive events use some form of tournament or rapid.

Until recently, the most popular time-limit for international tournaments was 40 moves in 2 hours, followed by 20 moves in 1 hour, followed by 30 minutes for all the remaining moves. These limits apply separately to each player, so the maximum length of a game under this time-limit is 7 hours. A time-limit of this sort can be used with both mechanical and electronic clocks, but since the latter have become almost universal in competitive play, new time-limits have been introduced which are only feasible with electronic clocks. These newer time-limits involve an **increment**, which is a certain amount of time added to your total each time you make a move, usually 30 seconds. If an increment is used, then it might apply from move one or only after a certain number of moves have been played. A typical time-limit of this type is 40 moves in 90 minutes and then 30 additional minutes to the end of the game with an increment of 30 seconds per move starting from the first move. The main point is that owing to the wide variety of time-limits used, you should make sure that you understand what the time-limit is when you play in a competitive event.

Domestic tournaments and club events, which are often played in the evening or at weekends, use a similar type of time-limit but with reduced time allocations. A typical example is 36 moves in 90 minutes, and then 15 minutes plus an increment for the remainder of the game. With this time-limit, it is possible to play more than one game a day; weekend tournaments often have three games on Saturday and two games on Sunday.

The presence of an increment has an important effect in the last phase of the game. If there is no increment then you have to play a potentially unlimited number of moves in a fixed time. Thus, even with a winning position, you may lose on time because it is physically impossible to make the necessary moves. Some tournaments use special rules to prevent this from happening; for example, you may be able to claim a draw if you have a winning position but not enough time to win it. The use of an increment avoids this rather unjust possibility, but increments can only be used with electronic clocks and they can also cause problems with the tournament schedule, because one cannot guarantee that all the games will be finished by a specific time.

Rapid (sometimes called **quickplay**) games are much faster affairs, and the time-limit is normally very simple: typically you have to play all your moves in either 25 or 30 minutes. This allows a whole tournament consisting of six rounds to be played in a single day. The use of an increment could cause problems in an event with such a compressed schedule, so most rapid events do not use increments. When you are starting out, it's probably a good idea to first try some rapid events. You get several games in a day, and such events usually have several groups which are allocated according to **rating** (see below). This gives most players the chance to compete in an event appropriate to their own playing strength.

Blitz games are faster still, with each player having at most five minutes for the whole game. While this is one of the most popular forms of light-hearted chess, clubs often discourage it because of the wear and tear on their expensive chess clocks, and because the noise may disturb more serious games. As mentioned above, blitz is the most popular form of online chess.

In competitive games played at a tournament time-limit, it is compulsory to keep a record of the game. Pieces of paper specially laid out for recording chess games, called **score-sheets**, are usually provided at tournaments. As soon as you have made a move and pressed your clock, you should write your move down. Likewise, when your opponent makes a move you should write it down before starting to think about it. It is illegal under international rules to write your move down **before** you play it. Your score-sheet is your only record of how many moves have been played, and you have no other way to tell if you have played, for example, the 40 moves necessary in the first two hours. Thus it pays to make sure your score-sheet is accurate. The score-sheet may be used by the **arbiter** (a chess referee) if there is a dispute. Don't throw your score-sheet away; as explained above, it provides valuable information to help improve your game. It is usually not necessary to keep a score-sheet in a rapid game, and it is impossible in blitz.

It is advisable to arrive promptly for the start of the game, if only because a late arrival causes you to lose time on your clock and is irritating to the opponent, who may wonder whether you are coming at all. Until recently, it was possible to arrive up to an hour late for a game without suffering any penalty other than the loss of time, but this has now changed. In some international tournaments, if you are not present at the start of the game you are automatically defaulted, while others allow a 15-minute leeway. Once again, it pays to check on the precise rules for the event you are taking part in before planning your journey.

In most of the world, it is customary for tournament organizers to provide chess sets, boards, clocks, score-sheets, etc. However, in America some events operate on a more do-it-yourself basis, with the players required to bring their own equipment. If you are playing in America, check what is required before you start out.

These days almost all tournaments and most clubs forbid smoking, a development one can only applaud. In a few cases, the consumption of alcohol is also prohibited.

Most chess tournaments use the **Swiss system**, in which everybody plays through to the end of the event. The basis of this system is that, so far as possible, competitors with the same score play each other. The advantage of this system is that it can cope with a large number of participants. The other common system, used for most top-level tournaments, is the **round-robin** (or **all-play-all**) system, in which every player meets every other player. This is a fairer system, but can only cope with a small number of players. Relatively few chess tournaments use a knock-out system; few players want to travel to an event when they might have to go home again after one game. At world championship level, **matches** are common; in this case, the same two players meet each other in several games, with the colours being swapped from one game to the next. A common mistake of journalists is to use 'game' and 'match' interchangeably, when in chess they mean quite different things (they would never make this mistake when writing about tennis, of course).

There are various conventions and matters of etiquette involved in playing chess, but most of these are just common sense. It is normal to shake hands with your opponent at the start and end of each game; failure to do this is considered a serious insult and has led to some controversial incidents in international events. This has led FIDE (*Fédération Internationale des Échecs* – the international chess federation) to move towards making the handshake compulsory, although their rules are still not entirely clear. Otherwise, most of the conventions relate to not disturbing your opponent. You should not speak to your opponent during the game, except to resign, claim a win on time, offer, accept or decline a draw, or to indicate a claim for a draw under the threefold repetition or 50-move rules. After the game it is quite a different matter, and it is common to analyse the game with your opponent (called a **post-mortem**). It is generally considered acceptable to have a cup of coffee or chocolate bar at the board, but a three-course meal is definitely not on. Crunchy apples are a marginal case. Don't bang the pieces on the board or hit the

clock with unnecessary force; don't shake the table; don't gloat if
your opponent makes an error, etc. – all common sense. In general,
chess-players are well-behaved at the board – you may have heard
stories of poor behaviour in world championship matches, but these
are very much the exception. Not disturbing your opponent helps
create a good atmosphere and makes playing the game a more pleas-
ant experience for everybody.

You will find more experienced players are very concerned about
their **rating**. Most national chess federations operate a **rating system** in which a player's performance is measured on a numerical
scale and there is a global system administered by FIDE. We will
take the FIDE system, called the **Elo system** after its inventor, Pro-
fessor Elo, as an illustration. It currently runs from a low point of
1200 up to Magnus Carlsen, the current world number one, who has
a rating of 2813. The basis of the system is that when you play in a
tournament, your expected score is calculated from your rating and
the ratings of your opponents. If you exceed this expected score then
your rating goes up; if you fail to achieve the expected score then
your rating goes down. At certain intervals (currently every two
months) new rating lists are published, and the process repeats. The
FIDE rating system was originally intended only for international-
standard players, but has gradually been extended to lower and lower
levels, perhaps because FIDE charges a fee for each player on the list.

For most players, who will probably never have an international
rating, the systems run by national federations are of more interest.
Unfortunately, these systems are amazingly incompatible. A rating
of 2000 might mean one thing in one country, and something totally
different in another country. Until not so long ago, Germany even
had a system where the stronger the player, the lower the number
representing his rating. The English system at least runs in the same
direction as the Elo system, although the numbers involved are different; an English grading of 200 is equivalent to an Elo of 2200.
Even where the numbers appear roughly similar to those of the FIDE
system, there are significant discrepancies. For example, a US rating
of 2600 may be equivalent to between 2400 and 2500 on the FIDE
system (the extent of the discrepancy is disputed). However, there is a
gradual move towards making national systems compatible with the
FIDE system, so the level of confusion should diminish with time.

Rating systems provide a fairly objective way to measure and compare the performance of players. Of course, everybody likes to improve, so the publication of a new rating list acquires a special significance. For grandmasters, Elo ratings determine whether they get to play in prestigious (and lucrative) tournaments, so for them ratings are a serious matter. Even lower down the scale, it may decide whether you play in your club's first or second team. However, it is important not to become obsessed with ratings. The main thing is to enjoy chess and learn more about it, rather than worry about the result of every game and its effect on your rating. If you are improving, sooner or later it will be reflected in the numbers.

It is possible to gain various chess titles. The most prestigious titles are those awarded by FIDE: starting at the top, these are international grandmaster, international master and FIDE master, which correspond very roughly to Elo ratings of 2500, 2400 and 2300. There are additional titles which are restricted to women players. However, the detailed rules for acquiring these titles are too complex to go into here.

Further Material

In addition to analysing your games at home, you may like to indulge in some further reading about chess. Although there are a vast number of books about every aspect of chess, especially the openings, elementary books are relatively uncommon. The following can be recommended: *The Mammoth Book of Chess* by Graham Burgess (updated edition, Constable & Robinson, 2009) is a good bedtime book and excellent value for money. *How to Beat Your Dad at Chess* (Gambit, 1998) and *Chess Tactics for Kids* (Gambit, 2003), both by Murray Chandler, are also useful books. These, despite their titles, are not only aimed at young players.

When you move to a slightly more advanced level, books tend to focus on a particular area of chess. *Learn Chess Tactics* by John Nunn (Gambit, 2004) carries on from Chapter 5 of this book. Further material on the endgame may be found in *Understanding Chess Endgames* by John Nunn (Gambit, 2009), while *How to Build Your Chess Opening Repertoire* (Gambit, 2003) by Steve Giddins contains good general advice on how to choose which openings to play.

Games collections are useful reading. These are more entertaining if they contain biographical material as well as chess analysis. *The Life and Games of Mikhail Tal* (Everyman Chess, 1997), covers the career of one of the most brilliant players in chess history, who died in 1992. A more general book of classic games is *The Mammoth Book of the World's Greatest Chess Games* by Graham Burgess, John Emms and John Nunn (2nd edition, Robinson, 2004).

There are also a number of magazines devoted to chess, most of them appearing on a monthly basis. In Britain, *Chess* is the main magazine, while in the US, *Chess Life*, the official magazine of the US Chess Federation, is dominant. *New in Chess* is a highly-regarded English-language magazine produced in the Netherlands. There are numerous local magazines, especially in the US. However, printed chess magazines are under threat as most information is now available on the Internet, and people are unwilling to pay to receive information a month late which they could obtain immediately and for free.

Computer-related products appear thick and fast with new versions of the competing products appearing all the time. The most popular playing programs include the commercial products *Fritz*, *Rybka* and *Shredder*. There are also several free playing programs, which you can easily find with the aid of a search engine. The free programs are also very strong, but lack many of the bells and whistles of the commercial products. The *Fritz and Chesster* series is an innovative software product aimed at teaching young players the basics of chess.

Conclusion

Chess has been played for at least 1400 years and has already endured far longer than the (Western) Roman Empire. During this vast span of time it has captivated people of many different cultures, and continues to do so today. The Internet makes it possible to communicate across the world as easily as making a local phone call, but there are still barriers of language and creed to surmount. The universal language of chess can, in a small way, help to bring people closer together.

On a personal level, chess is a fascinating pastime, which can prove both entertaining and rewarding. I have been playing for 50 years, and every day I spend some time on chess. It is my wish that you will obtain as much pleasure from the game as I have.